Beyond the Best Interests of the Child

New Edition with Epilogue

Beyond the Best Interests of the Child

New Edition with Epilogue

JOSEPH GOLDSTEIN
Law School, Yale University

ANNA FREUD
Hampstead Child-Therapy Clinic

ALBERT J. SOLNIT
Child Study Center, Yale University

THE FREE PRESS
A Division of Macmillan Publishing Co., Inc.
New York

COLLIER MACMILLAN PUBLISHERS
London

Copyright © 1973, 1979 by The Free Press
                    A Division of Macmillan Publishing Co., Inc.

The Free Press
A Division of Macmillan Publishing Co., Inc.
866 Third Avenue, New York, N.Y. 10022

Collier Macmillan Canada, Ltd.

Library of Congress Catalog Card Number: 79-7630

Printed in the United States of America

printing number
1 2 3 4 5 6 7 8 9 10

Library of Congress Cataloging in Publication Data

Goldstein, Joseph.
  Beyond the best interests of the child.

  Includes bibliographical references and index.
  1. Child welfare. 2. Children--Legal status,
laws, etc. I. Freud, Anna   joint
author. II. Solnit, Albert J., joint author.
III. Title.
KF547.G65 1979   362.7   79-7630
ISBN 0-02-912200-7
ISBN 0-02-912190-6 pbk.

Ann Landers's correspondence (see pages 140 and 141) is
reproduced from *The New Haven Register* by permission
of Ann Landers and Publishers-Hall Syndicate, Chicago.

The article concerning the Desramault Case (see pages 154
and 155) is reproduced from *The Times* (London) by permission.

Contents

Preface

It happens often enough that two authors join forces in producing a publication in which their individual contributions are inextricably intermingled. It is much less frequent for three people to embark on such a task and to achieve a result which does justice to each writer yet creates the final impression of a unified whole. To observe such a venture from its inception is an unusual privilege which I enjoyed.

The three authors of this volume are authorities in their particular fields, though each has on previous occasions applied his specialized knowledge in collaborations with colleagues in adjacent fields. They are also representative of three different institutions, the Yale Law School, the Hampstead Child-Therapy Clinic, London, and the Child Study Center, Yale University.

The impact of the Law School was obvious in the choice of the problem—the criticism of the existing laws governing the disposal of children and the attempt to formulate a revised code. Experience gained in the Hampstead Clinic was condensed in the chapters and paragraphs defining the relations between children and their adult environment, as well as in many items dealing with their changing needs during the period of growth and development. The Child Study Center contributed a wealth of clinical experience gained from actual cases of broken families, displaced children, and mishandled decisions about their fate.

Observing the three authors at their work, I was most fascinated by those moments when individual opinions clashed and lively battles ensued during which each contributor obstinately clung to and defended a conviction of his own. Objections of this kind sometimes concerned minor points of mere terminology, such as the new use of the expression "wanted child," which might lead to misunderstanding; at other times they raged around such vital issues as the complete abrogation of the biological parents' rights whenever these run counter to the child's welfare. But even disagreements which at first appeared insoluble were resolved after much discussion and argumentation and, sometimes, after an intervening night's sleep. In any event, the high excitement revealed the enormous investment in their joint venture and mutual collaboration. At moments of tension the atmosphere was also relieved by humor, for example, when one of them to his surprise discovered that what he stressed had not been forgotten and completely neglected; when another remembered nostalgically how easy and comfortable it had been to write books all on her own; or when at a point of rare agreement somebody remarked that their concerted action sounded to him like that of a symphony orchestra.

What I witnessed, finally, was the emergence of the benevolent figure of an enlightened judge who in his person embodied the knowledge and many personal characteristics of the three authors, i.e., sound knowledge of the law combined with the hard-won psychoanalytic knowledge of child development.

The idea for a book was first discussed in 1969 when plans were made for a series of individual essays to be contributed and signed by each of the authors. At the next meeting in 1970 at Yale, New Haven, this plan was scrapped in favor of the present sequence which presents the basic concepts and definitions, guidelines, and their applications. The common work continued at Rathmore near Baltimore, Eire and Maresfield Gardens, Hampstead, London, where the final working over took place in 1973. The fictitious New Haven-Hampstead Court bears witness to two of these locations, while the name of Baltimore given to the Judge is a reminder of the third.

DOROTHY BURLINGHAM

Acknowledgments

In the preparation of this book many individuals and several institutions have encouraged and facilitated our efforts. We wish to acknowledge our appreciation for this support.

For critical comment on various drafts of the manuscript: Laura C. Coddling, Steven Goldberg, Sonja Goldstein, Hillary Rodham.

For their assistance: Alexander M. Bickel, Robert Burt, Marshall Cohen, L. de Jong, John Hart Ely, Max Gitter, John Griffiths, Jay Katz, Seymour L. Lustman, Sally A. Provence, Amos Shapiro, Martha Solnit.

For encouragement and a peaceful atmosphere in which to work: Kingman Brewster, Jr., President, Yale University; Abraham S. Goldstein, Dean, Law School, Yale University; John Perry Miller, Director, Institution for Social and Policy Studies, Yale University.

For library assistance: Robert E. Brooks, Gene Coakley, James M. Golden, Isaiah Shein, Charles S. Smith.

For permission to reproduce provisions of the Uniform Marriage and Divorce Act, the Uniform Child Custody Jurisdiction Act, and the Revised Uniform Adoption Act: the National Conference of Commissioners on Uniform State Laws.

For financial assistance (travel, study, and research grants): the Field Foundation, the Ford Foundation, the Foundation for Research in Psychoanalysis, the Freud Centenary Fund, the Anna Freud Foundation, the Grant Foundation, the Institution for Social and Policy Study, the Andrew Mellon Foundation, the National Institute for Mental Health, and the New-Land Foundation.

For secretarial assistance: Yvonne M. Bowkett, Billie Hutching, Geraldine Formica, Gina Lewis, Sophie Powell, Elizabeth H. Sharp, Jean Yurczyk.

For creative and firm editing: Lottie M. Newman.

Part One

The Problem and Our Premises

Chapter 1

Child Placement in Perspective

The child is singled out by law, as by custom, for special attention. The law distinguishes between adult and child in physical, psychological, and societal terms. Adults are presumed to be responsible for themselves and capable of deciding what is in their own interests. Therefore, the law is by and large designed to safeguard their right to order their personal affairs free of government intrusion. Children, on the other hand, are presumed to be incomplete beings who are not fully competent to determine and safeguard their interests. They are seen as dependent and in need of direct, intimate, and continuous care by the adults who are personally committed to assume such responsibility. Thus, the state seeks to assure each child membership in a family with at least one such adult whom the law designates "parent."

Child placement laws are society's response to the

"success" or "failure" of a family in providing its children with an environment which adequately serves their needs. The degree of state intervention on the private ordering of the parent-child relationship ranges from a minimum—automatic assignment of a child by birth certificate to his biological parents—to a maximum—court-ordered removal of a child from his custodians because he is found to be "neglected" or "delinquent" or they are found "unfit" to be parents. The traditional goal of such interventions is to serve "the best interests of the child." In giving meaning to this goal, decisionmakers in law have recognized the necessity of protecting a child's physical well-being as a guide to placement. But they have been slow to understand and to acknowledge the necessity of safeguarding a child's psychological well-being. While they make the interests of a child paramount over all other claims when his physical well-being is in jeopardy, they subordinate, often intentionally, his psychological well-being to, for example, an adult's right to assert a biological tie. Yet both well-beings are equally important, and any sharp distinction between them is artificial.*

While we do not minimize the significance of the law's efforts to safeguard each child's bodily needs, our emphasis in this volume, due to the state of the law, is exclusively on the child's psychological needs. To that

---

* Law and social practice have been uneven in responding to the evolving meaning of childhood. The artificial distinction between physical and psychological well-being is a relic of the past in which adults viewed children more as chattel than as persons in their own right.[1]

end we have used psychoanalytic theory to develop generally applicable guidelines to child placement. These guidelines are intended to provide a basis for critically evaluating and revising the procedure and substance of court decisions, as well as statutes. They are to provide a theoretical and conceptual framework not only for exposing unsound practices and precedents, but also for understanding and making secure many sound, but frequently unfollowed decisions—many of which were arrived at intuitively long before psychoanalysis.[2]

"Child placement," for our purposes, is a term which encompasses all legislative, judicial, and executive decisions generally or specifically concerned with establishing, administering, or rearranging parent-child relationships. The term covers a wide range of variously labeled legal procedures for deciding who should be assigned or expected to seize the opportunity and the task of being "parent" to a child. These procedures include birth certification, neglect, abandonment, battered child, foster care, adoption, delinquency, youth offender, as well as custody in annulment, separation, and divorce. These labels, in many ways reminiscent of the stultifying common-law forms of action, have tended to obscure for scholar, draftsman, and practitioner a problem common to all such procedures. The crucial problem is how and to what extent the law can, through the manipulation of a child's external environment, protect his physical growth and emotional development.

How, the question then becomes, can the law assure for each child a chance to be a member of a family where he feels wanted and where he will have the opportunity, on a continuing basis, not only to receive and return affection, but also to express anger and to learn to manage his aggression? The law's answer is easy, automatic, and made with confidence if at birth the child is wanted by the adults who conceived him. But when, between birth and adulthood, a child's placement is in dispute and subject to competing and conflicting adult interests, the law finds the answer more difficult. It is confronted with a highly complex decision which involves, implicitly if not explicitly, a prediction about who, among available alternatives, holds most promise for meeting the child's psychological needs.

Psychoanalytic theory confirms the substantial limitations on our capacity to make such a prediction. Yet it provides a valuable body of generally applicable knowledge about a child's needs, knowledge which may be translated into guidelines to facilitate making decisions that inevitably must be made. It establishes, for example, as do developmental studies by students of other orientations, the need of every child for unbroken continuity of affectionate and stimulating relationships with an adult. That knowledge casts doubt upon adoption procedures which may leave the new child-parent relationship uncertain for years and upon divorce procedures which leave that relationship uncertain throughout childhood since custody decisions remain subject to court modification. It calls into question those custody decisions which split a child's placement between two parents or which provide the noncustodial parent with the right to visit or to force the child to visit. Such official invitations to erratic changes and discontinuity in the life of a child are but illustrative of many determinations in law which run contrary to the often professed purpose of the decisions themselves—to serve the best interests of the child.

In sum, this volume focuses on the development of guidelines to decisionmaking in law concerned with the selection and manipulation of a child's external environment as a means of improving and nourishing his internal environment. We examine and give functional definitions to the concepts of wanted child, and biological, psychological, adoptive, foster, and "common-law-adoptive" parent-child relationships. Alert to the limits of law and of our knowledge, we translate what we know from psychoanalysis about growth and development into procedural and substantive guidelines for deciding a child's placement. Finally, we apply our guidelines to rewriting actual judicial decisions and to drafting provisions for a model child placement statute.

We end this beginning with stating two value preferences which the authors share. First, we take the view that the law must make the child's needs paramount. This preference reflects more than our professional commitment. It is in society's best interests. Each time the cycle of grossly inadequate parent-child relationships is broken, society stands to gain a person capable of becoming an adequate parent for children of the future. Second, we have a preference for privacy. To safeguard the right of parents to raise their children as they see fit, free of government intrusion, except in cases of neglect and abandonment, is to safeguard each child's need for continuity. This preference for minimum state

intervention and for leaving well enough alone is rein-
forced by our recognition that law is incapable of effectively managing, except in a very gross sense, so delicate
and complex a relationship as that between parent and
child. Thus, this volume focuses primarily on contested
child placements: where the adults involved are unable
to reach agreement among themselves and resort to the
legal process for a resolution of their disputes.

Chapter 2

The Child–Parent Relationships

Children are presumed by law to be incomplete beings during the whole period of their development. Their inability to provide for their own basic needs, or even to maintain life without extraneous help, justifies their being automatically assigned by birth certificate to their biological parents or, where this natural relationship fails to function, by later court proceedings to parent substitutes. This intimate group of adults and their children constitutes the central core of a family. Responsibility for the child, for his survival, for his physical and mental growth, for his eventual adaptation to community standards, thus becomes that of the designated adults in a family to whom the child, in his turn, is responsive and accountable.

The legal status of the child is matched on the

psychological side by a number of tenets. A child's mental reliance on the adult world is at least as long-lived as his physical dependency. Each child's development unfolds in response to the environmental influences to which he is exposed. His emotional, intellectual, and moral capacities prosper, not in a void, and not without conflict, within his family relationships, and these determine his social reactions.

There are many pediatricians, nurses, health visitors, social workers, probation officers, nursery school workers, school teachers, and child therapists who agree with these findings and conclude from them that no child should be approached, assessed, treated, nursed, taught, or corrected without the parental influences being taken into account. They believe that without knowledge of the parents' influence neither the child's developmental successes and failures nor his social adjustments and maladjustments can be seen in their true light.

However valuable these insights are within the general context of psychoanalytic child psychology, if used by themselves they are misleading and highlight one side of child development while they obscure another. The problem is that some workers in the child care services have learned the lesson of environmental influence too well. Consequently they view the child as a mere adjunct to the adult world, a passive recipient of parental impact. They tend to ignore that children interact with the environment on the basis of their individual innate characteristics. It is this interaction, not mere response, which accounts for the countless variations in character and personality, as well as for the marked differences between siblings growing up in the same family. To see children too one-sidedly as mirroring their backgrounds blinds the observer to the uniqueness of their vital characteristics on which their own specific developmental needs are based. Yet, whatever their individual differences, the mental makeup of children generally differs from that of adults in the following respects:

Unlike adults, whose psychic functioning proceeds on more or less fixed lines, children change constantly, from one state of growth to another. They change with regard to their understanding of events, their tolerance for frustration, and their needs for and demands on motherly and fatherly care for support, stimulation, guidance, and restraint. These demands vary as the child matures and begins to need independence, i.e., gradual freedom from control. Since none of the child's needs remains stable, what serves his developmental interests on one level may be detrimental to his progression on another.

Unlike adults, who measure the passing of time by clock and calendar, children have their own built-in time sense, based on the urgency of their instinctual and emotional needs. This results in their marked intolerance for postponement of gratification or frustration, and an intense sensitivity to the length of separations.

Unlike adults, who are generally able to see occurrences in a relatively realistic perspective, young children experience events in an egocentric manner, i.e., as happening solely with reference to their own persons. Thus, they may experience, for example, the mere move from one house or location to another as a grievous loss, imposed on them; the birth of a sibling as an act of parental hostility; the emotional preoccupation or illness of a parent as rejection; the death of a parent as intentional abandonment.*

Unlike adults, who are generally better able to deal with the vagaries of life via reason and intellect, children are governed in much of their functioning by the irrational parts of their minds, i.e., their primitive wishes and impulses. Consequently, they respond to any threat to their emotional security with fantastic anxieties, denial, or distortion of reality, reversal or displacement of feelings—reactions which are no help for coping, but rather put them at the mercy of events.

Unlike adults, who are generally capable of maintaining positive emotional ties with a number of different individuals, unrelated or even hostile to each other, children lack the capacity to do so. They will freely love more than one adult only if the individuals in question feel positively to one another. Failing this, children become prey to severe and crippling loyalty conflicts.

Unlike adults, children have no psychological conception of relationship by blood-tie until quite late in their development. For the biological parents, the facts of having engendered, borne, or given birth to a child produce an understandable sense of preparedness for proprietorship and possessiveness. These considerations carry no weight with children who are emotionally unaware of the events leading to their births. What registers

---

* Similarly, their egocentricity makes them see other events as happening exclusively for their benefit.[1]

in their minds are the day-to-day interchanges with the adults who take care of them and who, on the strength of these, become the parent figures to whom they are attached.

Children then are not adults in miniature. They are beings per se, different from their elders in their mental nature, their functioning, their understanding of events, and their reactions to them. This effort to highlight the differences between adult and child, however, should not obscure the enormous variations in the quality and degree of such differences not only among different children but also in each individual child during the fluctuating course of his growth and development as a member of a family.

Families, too, both in function and membership may change through time and differ between cultures. Yet, the "family," however defined by society, is generally perceived as the fundamental unit responsible for and capable of providing a child on a continuing basis with an environment which serves his numerous physical and mental needs during immaturity. The law reflects this expectation about the family's relation to a child's well-being. The child's body needs to be tended, nourished, and protected. His intellect needs to be stimulated and alerted to the happenings in his environment. He needs help in understanding and organizing his sensations and perceptions. He needs people to love, receive affection from, and to serve as safe targets for his infantile anger and aggression. He needs assistance from the adults in curbing and modifying his primitive drives (sex and aggression). He needs patterns for identification provided by the parents, to build up a functioning moral conscience. As much as anything else, he needs to be accepted, valued, and wanted as a member of the family unit consisting of adults as well as other children.

Although all of these functions—if carried out by parents in a family setting—play their part in socializing the child, some of these functions serve this aim more directly than do others:

The parent who feeds the infant and puts him to bed thereby introduces a first compliance with a time schedule; the parents who grant but also withhold bodily and mental satisfactions help the child to realize that not all wishes can be fulfilled at all times. This increases the child's capacity to tolerate postponement of gratification and inevitable frustration.

The parents, by reacting to the child's behavior with appropriate praise and encouragement or criticism and discouragement, lay the first foundations for the child's own control of his drives and impulses, the lessening of his selfishness, and the beginning of consideration for others.

The parents represent a set of demands and prohibitions and attitudes toward work and community with which the child can identify.

Experiences with other children in the family strengthen the above capacities, enable the child to gain a sense of community, and provide additional opportunities for the child to form his conceptions of sharing, fair play, and justice.

This picture of the family is, however, an ideal one and is not often matched by reality. Children do not always develop according to their parents' expectation. There may be delays, deviations, and arrests in every aspect of their development, and each of these inevitably complicates the child's response to environmental influences. The family may make demands on the child which are legitimate objectively and the child may nevertheless, for subjective reasons, not be ready to comply. Thus, children in apparently well-functioning families may be ill-equipped to meet society's demands.

On the other hand, if families malfunction, the consequences for the child's social adaptation are many:

Physical care of the infant and toddler in the family may be as routinely and insensitively given as it is in an institution, or, conversely, may be exaggerated and exceed the child's normal needs. In neither case will it arouse the positive response which is the first primitive base for later social attitudes.

Parental involvement may be so minimal, even in a "complete" family, that the child's emotional demands remain unfulfilled.

Sibling involvement may be so minimal that the child does not learn to balance his own wishes against those of others.

The sexual identities of the parents may be insufficiently resolved so as to create confusion in the child about his own sexual identity.

Parents may provide the child with unsuitable models for identification.

Families may be incomplete. The prolonged absence or death of one parent may place the child at risk.[2] He is deprived of the benefits of a relationship with two adults who have an intimate relationship with each other. The family may be without other children, a situation which may make it more difficult for the child to acquire the give-and-take and sharing attitudes governing the peer community.

But where the family exerts its influence benevolently, with consideration, understanding, and compassion for each individual child member, the balanced opportunities for a unique development and for social adaptation are maximized. In such families—whether they develop out of biological, adoptive, foster, or common-law adoptive ties—the adults are the psychological parents and the children are wanted. It is on the meaning of these terms and concepts that we now focus.

THE BIOLOGICAL PARENT–CHILD RELATIONSHIP

The attributes "biological" or "natural" in common usage designate the parents who have actually produced the child. This so-called blood-tie gives them first right to the possession of the child. This claim which is confirmed by a birth certificate is not invalidated unless the child is found to be "neglected" or "delinquent" or unless the adults choose to give the child up for adoption or are found to be "unfit" as parents.[3]

Normally, the physical facts of having begotten a child or given birth to it have far-reaching psychological meaning for the parents as confirmation of their respective sexual identities, their potency and intactness. Derived from this is the inclusion of the newborn and infant in the parents' self-love. The overflow of this self-love to the child leads to the common parental overvaluation of their offspring. Biological parents are credited with an invariable, instinctively based positive tie to the child, although this is frequently belied by evidence to the contrary, in cases of infanticide, infant-battering, child neglect, abuse, and abandonment.

The biological parent's relationship to the child is seriously interfered with in instances where the adults in question reject their own male or female identity. When the newborn is defective, his very existence may become a reason for shame and guilt instead of pride, and for the father a discredit to his potency.

By contrast, for the child, the physical realities of his conception and birth are not the direct cause of his emotional attachment. This attachment results from day-to-day attention to his needs for physical care, nourishment, comfort, affection, and stimulation. Only a parent who provides for these needs will build a psychological relationship to the child on the basis of the biological one and will become his "psychological parent" in whose care the child can feel valued and "wanted." An absent biological parent will remain, or tend to become, a stranger.

THE PSYCHOLOGICAL PARENT–CHILD RELATIONSHIP

The child's psychological tie to a parent figure is not the simple, uncomplicated relationship which it may appear to be at first glance. While it is rooted inevitably in the infant's inability to ensure his own survival, it varies according to the manner in which protection is given and the physical needs fulfilled. Where this is done impersonally and with routine regularity, as in institutions, the infant may remain involved with his own body and not take an alert interest in his surroundings.* Where the adult in charge of the child is personally and emotionally involved, a psychological interplay between adult and child will be superimposed on the events of bodily care. Then the child's libidinal interest will be drawn for the first time to the human object in the outside world.

Such primitive and tenuous first attachments form the base from which any further relationships develop. What the child brings to them next are no longer only his needs for body comfort and gratification but his emotional demands for affection, companionship, and stimulating intimacy. Where these are answered reliably and regularly, the child-parent relationship becomes firm, with immensely productive effects on the child's intellectual and social development. Where parental care is inadequate, this may be matched by deficits in the child's mental growth. Where there are changes of parent figure or other hurtful interruptions, the child's vulnerability and the fragility of the relationship become evident. The child regresses along the whole line of his affections, skills, achievements, and social adaptation. It is only with the advance toward maturity that the emotional ties of the young will outgrow this vulnerability. The first relief in

---

* In extreme cases he even may lose or never develop an interest in his own body.[4]

this respect is the formation of internal mental images of the parents which remain available even if the parents are absent. The next step is due to identification with parental attitudes. Once these have become the child's own, they ensure stability within his inner structure.

As the prototype of true human relationship, the psychological child-parent relationship is not wholly positive but has its admixture of negative elements. Both partners bring to it the combination of loving and hostile feelings that characterize the emotional life of all human beings, whether mature or immature. The balance between positive and negative feelings fluctuates during the years. For children, this culminates in the inevitable and potentially constructive struggle with their parents during adolescence.

Whether any adult becomes the psychological parent of a child is based thus on day-to-day interaction, companionship, and shared experiences. The role can be fulfilled either by a biological parent or by an adoptive parent or by any other caring adult—but never by an absent, inactive adult, whatever his biological or legal relationship to the child may be.

The best qualities in an adult's personality give no assurance in themselves for a sound result if, for any reason, the necessary psychological tie is absent. Children may also be deeply attached to parents with impoverished or unstable personalities and may progress emotionally within this relationship on the basis of mutual attachment. Where the tie is to adults who are "unfit" as parents, unbroken closeness to them, and especially identification with them, may cease to be a benefit and become a threat. In extreme cases this necessitates state interference. Nevertheless, so far as the child's emotions are concerned, interference with the tie, whether to a "fit" or "unfit" psychological parent, is extremely painful.

THE WANTED CHILD

The psychological parent-child relationship remains incomplete if it is emotionally one-sided. That the parent is an essential figure for the child's feelings needs to be complemented by the child's figuring in a similar way in the parents' emotional life. Only a child who has at least one person whom he can love, and who also feels loved, valued, and wanted by that person, will develop a healthy self-esteem. He can then become confident of his own chances of achievement in life and convinced of his own human value. Where this positive environmental attitude toward an infant is missing from the start, the consequences become obvious in later childhood and adult life. They take the form of the individual's diminished care for the well-being of his own body, or for his physical appearance and clothing, or for his image presented to his fellow beings. What is damaged is his love and regard for himself, and consequently his capacity to love and care for others, including his own children.

Infants born as the result of an unwanted pregnancy are thus at risk from birth with an initially much reduced chance of healthy growth and development. Exceptions are those who do not remain unwanted after birth, but succeed in winning their parents' love by their mere existence, or those who are immediately placed with loving adults at birth.

Infants and children placed in institutions instead of being wanted in their own family, an adoptive or foster family, have an obvious disadvantage. Whatever beneficial qualities a psychological parent may be lacking, he offers the child the chance to become a wanted and needed member within a family structure; ordinarily this cannot happen even in the institutions where care, safety, and stimulation may be provided, but where the individual child has no psychological parents.

To be wanted ceases to be beneficial to the degree that "wanting" the child is not based on reciprocity of feelings and on recognition of the child's own personal characteristics. The child is placed in jeopardy whenever the adults' claim for him is based solely or predominantly on motives such as the wish to gain some financial advantage; to score over a warring partner after divorce; to force a reluctant sexual partner into marriage; to cement an insecure marital relationship; or to replace a child lost by death.

To be wanted also ceases to be beneficial if the adults' need for the child and valuation of him are excessive and if no or too little return from his side is expected. Such children do profit so far as their self-esteem is concerned. They become, if anything, too secure, self-content, and egotistical. They may also become ineducable in social respects since they are under no obligation to earn their parents' approval by curbing their own primitive impulses and wishes.

THE ADOPTIVE PARENT–CHILD RELATIONSHIP

The term "adoptive parent" designates an adult other than the biological parent to whom the state has assigned complete parental responsibility. Legal adoption cancels out the legal rights of the biological parents.[5] To safeguard their interests, even in cases where these run counter to the child's interests, either parental consent or abandonment is generally an essential preliminary to adoption in present-day law.[6]

Adoption in the early weeks of an infant's life gives the adoptive parents the biological parents' chance to develop a psychological parent-child relationship. This chance is diminished if adoption occurs at a later stage, after the infant or young child has had earlier placements, where he has formed and broken earlier attachments, or experienced separations. It is also diminished by the statutory requirement of a trial period before adoption is finalized. Due to the uncertainty of that situation, the parents may hesitate during this period to make a full commitment to the child.[7]

The facts of legal adoption are no guarantee that the adopting adults will become the psychological parents or that the adopted child will become a wanted child. This depends largely on the motivations for adopting, which range from the mere fact of being childless (for whatever reason) to the wish to replace a dead child, to acquire a companion for an only child, to rescue an orphaned or otherwise abandoned child, to have an heir, to stabilize a marriage, or to fulfill a conscious or unconscious fantasy. The capacity for parenthood may develop smoothly in the face of an infant's helplessness and dependence despite the fact that the preparation during the nine months of pregnancy is missing. Relationships may be negatively influenced when the presence of an adopted child constantly reminds the parents of their incapacity to produce children of their own.

Adoptive parents frequently wish that the adopted child will grow up in their own image, an attitude which may be reflected in statutory and adoption agencies' attempts to have children "matched" with prospective adopters so far as physical features, social background, and possible hereditary endowment are concerned.[8]

Adoption agencies advise that children be informed of their adoptive status. Such knowledge has a different impact at different ages. The young child tends to ignore it, even if informed repeatedly, and to develop his attachments as a wanted child to his psychological parents. The older child uses the information to a greater or lesser extent, depending on his developmental conflicts with his parents. Whenever he is disappointed in them or as he learns to appraise them realistically, the adoptive parents are compared with a fantasy image of the biological parents, however little these figured earlier in the child's mind. Adolescents frequently institute a search for the lost and unknown parents, as a step preliminary to achieving independence from any parental authority and reaching maturity.[9]

THE FOSTER PARENT–CHILD RELATIONSHIP

The term foster parent is in use for any adult who receives a child for "board and care" either from a state welfare commission or from a recognized social agency.[10]

The terms under which such assignments are made vary according to the amounts of financial compensation as well as according to the services expected. These services range from the purely physical and material to the psychological, such as the child "shall be given sufficient and suitable food, bed"; "opportunity to attend school, and attend religious services"; "receive medical care"; "shall not be required to perform an amount of labor unsuitable for his age and strength"; and "should receive all the emotional benefits of a true member of the new family." Further variations concern guidance being given as to visiting by the biological parents, granting of pocket money, arrangements for recreation or day-to-day activities.

Nevertheless, agreements generally made with foster parents are consistent in being emphatic on two main conditions:

that the child in question is placed on a *temporary* board and care basis only and not placed with the foster family for adoption;

that the welfare commissioner or agency reserve the right to remove the child at any time from the foster home and that upon such removal the initial agreement is canceled immediately.[11]

Adherence to these terms has unquestionable consequences for the child-foster parent relationship.

So far as the adults are concerned, it implies a warning against any deep emotional involvement with the child since under the given insecure circumstances this would be judged as excessive.[12] Also, they find them-

selves deprived of the position on which parental tolerance, endurance, and devotion are commonly based,
namely, that of being the undisputed sole possessor of
the child and the supreme arbiter of his fate. What is
left, apart from the conscientious fulfillment of a task
once taken over, is the appeal made by a helpless immature being on the mature adult's concern. This reaction
can be counted on in many instances, but, understandably enough, more often only for the infant and very
young child. This appeal is relatively absent in the older
child who is on the one hand less helpless and on the
other hand in many respects more troublesome.

So far as the foster child is concerned, he will, at
least after early infancy has passed, feel the imperma-
nency and insecurity of the arrangement which clashes
with his need for emotional constancy. He will feel himself in the care of parents who are by no means "omnip-
otent" but have no more than partial protective power
and control of his fate. If his biological parents visit, he
will find it difficult to react to two sets of parents for
more than a short period of time, its length depending on
the child's age and stage of psychological development.

In short, under the terms of the agreement, the
child-foster parent relationship has little likelihood of
promoting the psychological parent-wanted child relationship. This defeats the very intentions of the decision
to move from professional institutional care to family
care. Where foster parents heed the warning given and
fulfill their task with the reservations implied in a semi-
professional attitude, they evoke in the child a reduced

response as well, too lukewarm to serve the infant's developmental needs for emotional progress or the older child's need for relatedness and identification. Further, and this serves to explain the frequent breakdown of foster placement, the emotional bonds of the adults to the children will be loose enough to be broken whenever external circumstances make the presence of the foster child in the home inconvenient and irksome.

In another sense, fostering fails in cases where the adults transgress the role assigned to them, i.e., where their feelings become totally involved with the child in their care. With the child responding and feeling truly wanted, the adults advance from the status of foster parents to that of becoming psychological parents. Even though their applications for legal adoption may be denied in court, in fact what they may have become are parents by "common-law adoption," which, we would argue, deserves recognition.[13]

At present, foster parent placements are also used for those emergencies where children need to be cared for due to temporary incapacity of their parents, whether biological or adoptive, caused, for example, by accidents, illness, and confinements, or in special situations where there is a purpose such as "grooming for adoption." Obviously, with such short-term placements, no true parental task is involved and not even the limited parent-child attachment which makes fostering successful can be expected to develop. Where the child is merely held for others, special techniques have to be used, either to keep existing attachments alive in the child's mind or to prepare the way for future ones so far as this is possible.[14]

THE COMMON-LAW ADOPTIVE PARENT–CHILD RELATIONSHIP

The term "common-law adoptive parent" is not currently in use in law.[15] We use the term to designate those psychological parent-child relationships which develop outside of either placement by formal adoption or by the initial assignment of a child to his biological parents. Such relationships may develop when a parent, without resort to any legal process, leaves his or her child with a friend or relative for an extended period of time.[16] Further, as already indicated, foster parents in daily interaction with the child, and answering to the child's emotional involvement, may become totally involved on their side and appear before the courts pressing for the right to be considered adopters. Such claims are often disputed by the social agencies either on their own behalf or on that of the biological parents.

What is before the court in such instances is a situation where all the psychological elements implied in a parent-child relationship are present and functioning effectively. It is a state of affairs identical with a successful adoption in every sense except the legal sense—in fact, a "common-law adoption." Where legal recognition is withheld from it and the child removed, the forcible interruption of the relationship, besides causing distress to the fostering adults, is reacted to by the child with emotional distress and a setback of ongoing development. Such reactions do not differ from those caused by separation from, or death of, natural or adoptive parents.

On the basis of our knowledge from psychoanalysis and law we have sought in this chapter to define some basic terms and concepts out of which to construct guidelines for child placement. These guidelines are applicable to decisions concerned with such apparently diverse legal procedures as adoption, custody in divorce and separation, neglect and foster care.[17] As we turn to a formulation and discussion of these guidelines, it is important to emphasize that these concepts encompass highly complex relationships.[18] The terms will be useful only if they are carefully employed. They must not become shorthands which in any way obscure how intricate and delicate are the interpersonal processes we have sought to describe.

Part Two

Guidelines and Their Implications for the Laws of Child Placement

Chapter 3

On Continuity, a Child's Sense of Time, and the Limits of Both Law and Prediction

We propose three component guidelines for decision-makers concerned with determining the placement and the process of placement of a child in a family or alternative setting. These guidelines rest on the belief that children whose placement becomes the subject of controversy should be provided with an opportunity to be placed with adults who are or are likely to become their psychological parents.

PLACEMENT DECISIONS SHOULD SAFEGUARD THE CHILD'S NEED FOR CONTINUITY OF RELATIONSHIPS

Continuity of relationships, surroundings, and environmental influence are essential for a child's normal development. Since they do not play the same role in later life, their importance is often underrated by the adult world.

Physical, emotional, intellectual, social, and moral growth does not happen without causing the child inevitable internal difficulties. The instability of all mental processes during the period of development needs to be offset by stability and uninterrupted support from external sources. Smooth growth is arrested or disrupted when upheavals and changes in the external world are added to the internal ones.

Disruptions of continuity have different consequences for different ages:

In *infancy,* from birth to approximately 18 months, any change in routine leads to food refusals, digestive upsets, sleeping difficulties, and crying. Such reactions occur even if the infant's care is divided merely between mother and baby-sitter. They are all the more massive where the infant's day is divided between home and day care center; or where infants are displaced from the mother to an institution; from institutional to foster care; or from fostering to adoption. Every step of this kind inevitably brings with it changes in the ways the infant is handled, fed, put to bed, and comforted. Such moves from the familiar to the unfamiliar cause discomfort, distress, and delays in the infant's orientation and adaptation within his surroundings.

Change of the caretaking person for *infants and toddlers* further affects the course of their emotional development. Their attachments, at these ages, are as thoroughly upset by separations as they are effectively promoted by the constant, uninterrupted presence and attention of a familiar adult. When infants and young children find themselves abandoned by the parent, they not only suffer separation distress and anxiety but also setbacks in the quality of their next attachments, which will be less trustful. Where continuity of such relationships is interrupted more than once, as happens due to multiple placements in the early years, the children's emotional attachments become increasingly shallow and indiscriminate. They tend to grow up as persons who lack warmth in their contacts with fellow beings.

For *young children* under the age of 5 years, every disruption of continuity also affects those achievements which are rooted and develop in the intimate interchange with a stable parent figure, who is in the process of becoming the psychological parent. The more recently the achievement has been acquired, the easier it is for the child to lose it. Examples of this are cleanliness and speech. After separation from the familiar mother, young children are known to have breakdowns in toilet training and to lose or lessen their ability to communicate verbally.[1]

For *school-age children,* the breaks in their relationships with their psychological parents affect above all those achievements which are based on identification with the parents' demands, prohibitions, and social ideals. Such identifications develop only where attachments are stable and tend to be abandoned by the child if he feels abandoned by the adults in question. Thus, where children are made to wander from one environment to another, they may cease to identify with any set of substitute parents. Resentment toward the adults who have disappointed them in the past makes them adopt the attitude of not caring for anybody; or of making the new parent the scapegoat for the shortcomings of the former one. In any case, multiple placement at these ages puts many children beyond the reach of educational influence, and becomes the direct cause of behavior which the schools experience as disrupting and the courts label as dissocial, delinquent, or even criminal.[2]

With *adolescents,* the superficial observation of their behavior may convey the idea that what they desire is discontinuation of parental relationships rather than their preservation and stability. Nevertheless, this impression is misleading in this simple form. It is true that their revolt against any parental authority is normal developmentally since it is the adolescent's way toward establishing his own independent adult identity. But for a successful outcome it is important that the breaks and disruptions of attachment should come exclusively from his side and not be imposed on him by any form of abandonment or rejection on the psychological parents' part.

Adults who as children suffered from disruptions of continuity may themselves, in "identifying" with their many "parents," treat their children as they themselves were treated—continuing a cycle costly for both a new generation of children as well as for society itself.[3]

Thus, continuity is a guideline because emotional attachments are tenuous and vulnerable in early life and need stability of external arrangements for their development.

IMPLICATIONS

Some of the implications of this guideline for the laws on adoption, custody, and foster care are that each child placement be final and unconditional and that pending final placement a child must not be shifted to accord with each tentative decision. This means that all child placements, except where specifically designed for brief temporary care, shall be as permanent as the placement of a newborn with its biological parents.

ADOPTION

Once final, adoption is unconditional and thus accords with our continuity guideline. However, the usual waiting period of a year between a child's placement with the adopting family and the final order of adoption conflicts with this guideline. The "waiting period" is, as the name suggests, a period of uncertainty for adult and child. It is a period of probation encumbered by investigative visits and the fear of interruption. It is not, as it ought to be, a full opportunity for developing secure and stable attachments.

For the state, the waiting period may provide an opportunity to interrupt developing relationships for reasons that would not justify intrusion into any permanent parent-child relationship.[4] For some adopting parents the period may be one in which they place the child on "probation," an intolerable handicap for initiating such a delicate relationship. It may even provide a temptation for some adopting parents (and for some adopted children) not to allow the new relationship to develop.

Furthermore, for those families which at the time of adoption already include other children, the knowledge that the state can take the new child away is experienced as a threat. And in those cases where the fear or wish that the new brother or sister be taken away is actually realized, the detrimental impact on the health and well-being of the child who is already a member of the family is incalculable.

We propose, therefore, that the adoption decree be made final the moment a child is actually placed with the adopting family. To accord with the continuity guideline this would mean that the adoption order would be as final as a birth certificate, not subject to special supervision or open to special challenge by state or agency.*

The certainty of final placement should make all of the participants more aware than they often seem to be under current practice of the implications of the decisions to place a child for adoption and for a family to adopt a child. Moreover, as for all "final" placements, whether by birth certificate or adoption, "abuse," "neglect," and "abandonment," for example, could trigger state intervention. But even such placement proceedings must consider the continuity guideline in deciding whether an existing relationship should be altered. The advantages of continuing, ongoing "imperfect" relationships must be weighed even in neglect proceedings against those of the alternative placements that can be made available.

---

* If adopting parents change their minds, they could, as can biological parents, activate state processes designed to provide the child with another opportunity to be placed.[5]

Finally, it should be noted that all of the continuity problems attributable to the waiting period are exacerbated by the lengthy opportunity for appeal following a final decree. A disappointed party or a relinquishing adult who withdraws consent may, by seeking review, extend the uncertainty for years. We do not propose, as we do for the waiting period, that there be no period during which the right to appeal is protected. But the continuity guideline dictates that the period for appeal should be drastically shortened, a proposal we discuss later in relation to a guideline concerning the special meaning of time for a child.[6]

CUSTODY IN DIVORCE AND SEPARATION

Child placement in divorce and separation proceedings are never final and often are conditional. The lack of finality, which stems from the court's retention of jurisdiction over its custody decision, invites challenges by a disappointed party claiming changed circumstances. This absence of finality coupled with the concomitant increase in opportunities for appeal are in conflict with the child's need for continuity. As in adoption, a custody decree should be final, that is, not subject to modification.[7]

One reason for the retention of continuing jurisdiction by the court is that custody orders may be made on conditions such as a requirement to send a child to religious school, or to provide regular medical examinations. The obligation to enforce such conditions prompts interruption by disappointed parties who claim violation. In addition, certain conditions such as visitations may themselves be a source of discontinuity.[8] Children have difficulty in relating positively to, profiting from, and maintaining the contact with two psychological parents who are not in positive contact with each other. Loyalty conflicts are common and normal under such conditions and may have devastating consequences by destroying the child's positive relationships to both parents. A "visiting" or "visited" parent has little chance to serve as a true object for love, trust, and identification, since this role is based on his being available on an uninterrupted day-to-day basis.

Once it is determined who will be the custodial parent,[*] it is that parent, not the court, who must decide under what conditions he or she wishes to raise the child. Thus, the noncustodial parent should have no legally enforceable right to visit the child, and the custodial parent should have the right to decide whether it is desirable for the child to have such visits.[9] What we have said is designed to protect the security of an ongoing relationship—that between the child and the custodial parent. At the same time the state neither makes nor breaks the psychological relationship between the child and the noncustodial parent, which the adults involved may have jeopardized. It leaves to them what only they can ultimately resolve.[†] [10]

Even if all custody decisions were unconditional, the guideline of continuity would dictate another alteration of procedure. On appeal pending review of the final

---

[*] This determination may be made either by agreement between the divorcing parents or by the court in the event each claims custody.

[†] For further discussion of visitation, see Epilogue.

decision a child ought not to be shifted back and forth between competing claimants merely to accord with what may prove to be tentative decisions.[11]

FOSTER AND OTHER TEMPORARY PLACEMENTS

In foster or other less formal but temporary placements, the continuity guideline should prompt the development of procedures and opportunities in temporary placement for maintaining relationships between child and absent parent. Thus, unlike permanent placements, foster placements should be conditional.[12] This does not mean that foster parents are to remain aloof and uninvolved.[13] Nor does this mean that foster care is to be used as a means of keeping the child from establishing a positive tie with his "temporary" adult custodians by constantly shifting him from one foster setting to another in order to protect an adult's right of reclaim.[14] But once the prior tie has been broken, the foster or other temporary placements can no longer be considered temporary. They may develop into or substantially begin to become psychological parent-child relationships, which in accord with the continuity guideline deserve recognition as a common-law adoption.

The choice between adoption and long-term foster care is complex and involves many factors. One of them is the provision of financial help to foster parents,[15] whereas adoptive parents receive no subsidy. Thus, the recognition of common-law adoptions could be strengthened by providing for subsidized adoption[16] as an alternative to long-term foster care or institutionalization.

PLACEMENT DECISIONS SHOULD REFLECT THE CHILD'S, NOT THE ADULT'S, SENSE OF TIME

A child's sense of time, as an integral part of the continuity concept, requires independent consideration. That interval of separation between parent and child which would constitute a break in continuity for an infant, for example, would be of no or little significance to a school-age youngster. The time it takes to break an old or to form a new attachment will depend upon the different meanings time has for children at each stage of their development.

Unlike adults, who have learned to anticipate the future and thus to manage delay, children have a built-in time sense based on the urgency of their instinctual and emotional needs. As an infant's memory begins to incorporate the way in which parents satisfy wishes and needs, as well as the experience of the reappearance of parents after their disappearance, a child gradually develops the capacity to delay gratification and to anticipate and plan for the future.

Emotionally and intellectually an infant and toddler cannot stretch his waiting more than a few days without feeling overwhelmed by the absence of parents. He cannot take care of himself physically, and his emotional and intellectual memory is not sufficiently matured to enable him to use thinking to hold on to the parent he has lost. During such an absence for the child under two years of age, the new adult who cares for the child's physical needs is latched onto "quickly"* as the potential

---

* We should be alert to the fact that time words such as "quickly" express an adult's sense of time. Were the infant to write

psychological parent. The replacement, however ideal, may not be able to heal completely, without emotional scarring, the injury sustained by the loss.[17]

For most children under the age of five years, an absence of parents for more than two months is equally beyond comprehension. For the younger school-age child, an absence of six months or more may be similarly experienced. More than one year of being without parents and without evidence that there are parental concerns and expectations is not likely to be understood by the older school-aged child and will carry with it the detrimental implications of the breaches in continuity we have already described. After adolescence is fully launched an individual's sense of time closely approaches that of most adults.

Thus, the child's sense of the passage of time depends on what part of the mind does the measuring. It may be either the sensible, reasoning part which accepts the laws of the external world, or the impulsive, egocentric part which ignores the surroundings and is exclusively bent on seeking pleasurable satisfaction. The young child starts in the latter way, with his impulses being incapable of tolerating delay and waiting. Postponement of action and the foreseeing of consequences are introduced very gradually in step with the maturing of the personality. A child will experience a given time period not according to its actual duration, measured objectively by calendar and clock, but according to his purely subjective feelings of impatience and frustration.

---

the sentence in the text it would read "latched onto after a *prolonged period* of time."

These will decide whether the intervals set for feeding, or for the absence of the mother, or the duration of hospitalization, etc., will seem to the child short or long, tolerable or intolerable, and as a result, will prove harmless or harmful in their consequences.

The significance of parental absences depends, then, upon their duration, frequency, and the developmental period during which they occur. The younger the child, the shorter is the interval before a leave-taking will be experienced as a permanent loss accompanied by feelings of helplessness and profound deprivation. Since a child's sense of time is directly related to his capacity to cope with breaches in continuity, it becomes a factor in determining if, when, and with what urgency the law should act.

IMPLICATIONS

The child's-sense-of-time guideline would require decisionmakers to act with "all deliberate speed" to maximize each child's opportunity either to restore stability to an existing relationship or to facilitate the establishment of new relationships to "replace" old ones. Procedural and substantive decisions should never exceed the time that the child-to-be-placed can endure loss and uncertainty.

The courts, social agencies, and all the adults concerned with child placement must greatly reduce the time they take for decision. While the taking of time is often correctly equated with care, reasoned judgment, and the assurance of fairness, it often also reflects too large and burdensome caseloads or inefficiently deployed resources.

Whatever the cause of the time-taking, the costs as well as the benefits of the delay to the child must be weighed. Our guideline would allow for no more delay than that required for reasoned judgment. By reasoned judgment we do not mean certainty of judgment. We mean no more than the most reasonable judgment that can be made within the time available—measured to accord with the child's sense of time. Therefore, to avoid irreparable psychological injury, placement, whenever in dispute, must be treated as the emergency that it is for the child.*

The procedures of child placement are not designed to assure a prompt final decision. The process is characterized by extended periods of uncertainty caused by overcautious and overworked administrative agencies; by courts with overcrowded dockets, extended and oft-postponed hearings; and by judges who are inclined to procrastinate before rendering their decisions at trial or on appeal.[18] Yet when the *physical* well-being of a child or adult may be endangered by delay or when delay may cause irreparable injury to the national security or to a person's right to an education, property or the free exercise of speech, both administrative and judicial bodies have demonstrated their capacity, if not their obligation, to make prompt and final determinations.[19] When, for example, parents refuse to authorize a blood transfusion for their deathly ill child, hospitals and courts can and do move with great dispatch and flexibility by giving such cases priority. Judges may act in a matter of hours after an application for decision is made—they may even

---

* Three months may not be a long time for an adult decisionmaker. For a young child it may be forever.

conduct their hearings at bedside in the hospital.[20] The blood transfusion cases may be perceived as emergency child placement cases for a temporary period and a limited purpose. But the model of a procedural scheme for treating all child placements as emergencies may more readily be taken from another setting. In order to avoid irreparably jeopardizing a motion picture exhibitor's constitutional right to freedom of expression, the U.S. Supreme Court wrote as follows:

> To this end, the exhibitor must be assured . . . that the censor will within a specified brief period either issue a license or go to court to restrain showing the film. Any restraint imposed in advance of a final determination on the merits must similarly be limited to preservation of the status quo for the shortest fixed period compatible with sound judicial resolution. . . .[21]

Were the court to adopt this position to safeguard a child's psychological health, it would have to say:

> To this end, the child must be assured that the placement agency will in a specified brief period either decide not to challenge the current placement, or go to court to arrange a new placement. Any temporary placement imposed in advance of a final determination on the merits must similarly be limited to preservation of the status quo for the shortest fixed period compatible with sound judicial resolution.

We propose, then, that as a matter of normal procedure a child's placement be treated by agency and court as a matter of urgency which gives consideration to a child's sense of time by granting such cases a high priority, by dealing with them rapidly, and by accelerating the course of review and final decision.

ADOPTION

For adoption agencies such a procedural scheme would mean pursuing a policy of early placements. Infants should, if possible, be placed even before birth. Expectant parents who contemplate putting their child up for adoption should receive agency assistance in reaching a firm decision before birth, either to keep or not to keep the child. Adopting families should be investigated and selected in advance of a child's availability of adoption. If anyone is to be kept waiting, it should not be the child, but the adults for whom the anticipation may be a positive factor. Before placement, there should not be prolonged periods of observation for gathering information about the newborn in order to certify its physical and intellectual fitness. Adopting families should be prepared to accept the "adopted" child the moment it becomes available. We share the view of Littner, who observed:

> There is no question that the longer we wait, the more we will know. Yet . . . to be able to give complete assurance of normal development we would have to place adults, and not children. [F]or the majority of adopted children, extra in-

formation that would come from waiting would *not* have resulted in a different placement. [A]ny program that does not place children early is running the risk of exposing the majority of their children to certain perils of late placement in order to protect the minority from the possible dangers of misplacement.[22]

Of course, the older a child is at the time of adoption, the longer the delay may be to find a placement which will maximize continuity of environment including life style, relationships with siblings, and educational opportunities.

As for court procedures in adoption, initial hearings should be promptly scheduled and decisions rendered quickly. The period for appeal should be extremely short, not more than a week or two with a final decision rendered within days after the close of that hearing. Prompt appeal and decision safeguard not only the interest of the child but also those of aggrieved adult parties. If the continuity guideline is to be observed by the court, the longer a child remains with the adult who retains custody pending appeal, the less likely are the chances for an aggrieved party, even if right in principle, to obtain custody.

SEPARATION AND DIVORCE

All that has been said with regard to judicial proceedings in adoption applies as well to child custody in divorce or separation. The child's-sense-of-time guideline would require that all disputes between the parents about the placement of their children be resolved by separate and accelerated proceedings prior to and without waiting for a determination on the merits of the divorce or separation action itself. An aggrieved party's right to appeal the custody decision must be exercised shortly after the initial award with a hearing and final decision by the appellate court to be rendered not more than a few weeks later. Such placement decisions become final, then, as a result of the appellate review or at the expiration of the time for appeal. To accord with our continuity guideline it must in no way be contingent upon the ultimate outcome of the divorce or separation action.[23]

We have not attempted to lay down rigid time limits for administrative or judicial decisions in adoption, divorce, or separation placements. Rather we have sought only to suggest for legislative consideration a possible procedural design which would be sensitive and responsive to a child's differing sense of time.[24]

ABANDONMENT AND NEGLECT

The concept of abandonment or permanent neglect, to turn from procedure to substance, provides another illustration for the application of our guidelines. The law of abandonment, in determining, for example, the eligibility of a child for adoption, rests primarily on the intent of the neglecting parent, not on the duration of his or her absence.[25] It may even rest on how diligent a child care agency has been in its efforts "to encourage and strengthen" the relationship between a child in foster care and the absent biological parent.[26] The failure of an agency to make such an effort can preclude a court from finding that a child has been abandoned in law even though he has been abandoned psychologically for many years.[27]

To the extent that time is a factor, whatever the age of the child, not less than one year of neglect is generally required to establish the requisite personal intent to abandon.[28] Moreover, abandonment has been perceived as a continuing process which may be reversed by the absent parent's express declaration of a change of mind.[29]

Application of the child's-sense-of-time guideline would require a shift of focus to the individual child's tolerance of absence and sense of abandonment and away from the adult's intent to abandon or an agency's failure to encourage a relationship. Furthermore, rather than a statutory one-year period, the time factor would be flexible and vary with a child's maturity at the time of separation, and the extent to which the ties with the absent adults have effectively been kept alive.

The process through which a new child-parent status emerges is too complex and subject to too many individual variations for the law to provide a rigid statutory timetable.* For the purposes of declaring a child eligible for adoption or of acknowledging the existence of a common-law adoptive relationship, abandonment in law would have taken place by the time the parents' absence has caused the child to feel no longer wanted by them. It would be that time when the child, having felt helpless and abandoned, has reached out to establish a new relationship with an adult who is to become or has become his psychological parent.[30]

* For modification of this position see Chapter 4 of *Before the Best Interests of the Child* (Free Press, 1979).

A statute may provide that a finding of abandonment may rest upon evidence that so much time has elapsed from the child's vantage point that the biological or adoptive tie never matured into a psychological tie with the absent adult, or that the developing psychological tie has been broken or damaged and that the child needs to or has already begun to develop a new relationship with another adult. Such a statute would include a presumption that (barring extraordinary efforts to maintain the continuity of a "temporarily interrupted" relationship), the younger the child, the shorter the period of relinquishment before a developing psychological tie is broken and a new relationship has begun. Abandonment or permanent neglect would then be defined to comport with a child's sense of time.

CHILD PLACEMENT DECISIONS MUST TAKE INTO ACCOUNT THE LAW'S INCAPACITY TO SUPERVISE INTERPERSONAL RELATIONSHIPS AND THE LIMITS OF KNOWLEDGE TO MAKE LONG-RANGE PREDICTIONS

Though obvious once said, when left unsaid, the limitations of law often go unacknowledged in discussions about child placement. Too frequently there is attributed to law and its agents a magical power—a power to do what is far beyond its means. While the law may claim to establish relationships, it can in fact do little more than give them recognition and provide an opportunity for them to develop. The law, so far as specific individual relationships are concerned, is a relatively crude instru-

ment.[31] It may be able to destroy human relationships;
but it does not have the power to compel them to develop.
It neither has the sensitivity nor the resources to maintain or supervise the ongoing day-to-day happenings between parent and child—and these are essential to meeting ever-changing demands and needs.[32] Nor does it have
the capacity to predict future events and needs, which
would justify or make workable over the long run any
specific conditions it might impose concerning, for example, education, visitation, health care, or religious up-
bringing. We share the view—one which is too easily
ignored in the law and administration of child placement
—of Justice Wachenfeld:

> The uncertainties of life . . . will always
> remain to be encountered as long as one lives. . . .
> Their devious forms and variations are too com-
> plicated and numerous to be susceptible of tabu-
> lation. Our inability to predict or solve them
> anchors us closely to nature's intendment. . . .
> A judicial approach does not make the
> future more readily foreseeable and the assurance
> of our decisions, whatever it be, is unfortunately
> circumscribed by the frailties of human judg-
> ment.[33]

The law, then, ought to and generally does prefer
the private ordering of interpersonal relationships over
state intrusions on them.[34]

Yet the law does intrude. When it does, it becomes important for decisionmakers to be guided by an

understanding of the limitations not only of the legal process but also of the predictive value of the knowledge on which its judgments can be based. Each child placement, even that by birth certificate, is based upon assumptions and predictions about children and the adults who are designated parents. As the continuity and the child's-sense-of-time guidelines suggest, placement decisions can be based on certain generally applicable and useful predictions. We can, for example, identify who, among *presently available* adults, is or has the capacity to become a psychological parent and thus will enable a child to feel wanted. We can predict that the adult most likely suited for this role is the one, if there be one, with whom the child has already had and continues to have an affectionate bond rather than one of otherwise equal potential who is not yet in a primary relationship with the child. Further, we can predict that the younger the child and the more extended the period of uncertainty or separation, the more detrimental it will be to the child's well-being and the more urgent it becomes even without perfect knowledge to place the child permanently.

Beyond these, our capacity to predict is limited.[35] No one—and psychoanalysis creates no exception—can forecast just what experiences, what events, what changes a child, or for that matter his adult custodian, will actually encounter.[36] Nor can anyone predict in detail how the unfolding development of a child and his family will be reflected in the long run in the child's personality and character formation. Thus the law will not act in the child's interests but merely add to the uncertainties if it tries to do the impossible—guess the future and impose on the custodian special conditions for the child's care. This merely leads to harmful and threatening discontinuity by leaving the decision for placement open and subject to special challenges by someone who claims that conditions have so changed that the custodian should be replaced. In the long run, the child's chances will be better if the law is less pretentious and ambitious in its aim, that is, if it confines itself to the avoidance of harm and acts in accord with a few, even if modest, generally applicable short-term predictions.

Chapter 4

On the Least Detrimental Alternative

*PLACEMENTS SHOULD PROVIDE THE LEAST
DETRIMENTAL AVAILABLE ALTERNATIVE FOR
SAFEGUARDING THE CHILD'S GROWTH AND
DEVELOPMENT*

As an overall guideline for child placement we propose, instead of the "in-the-best-interests-of-the-child" standard, "the least detrimental available alternative for safeguarding the child's growth and development." The new standard has as its major components the three guidelines which we have already described. The least detrimental alternative, then, is that specific placement and procedure for placement which maximizes, in accord with the child's sense of time and on the basis of short-term predictions given the limitations of knowledge, his or her opportunity for being wanted and for maintaining on a continuous basis a relationship with at least one adult who is or will become his psychological parent.

Even though we agree with the manifest purpose of the "in-the-best-interests-of-the-child" standard, we adopt a new guideline for several reasons. First, the traditional standard does not, as does the phrase "least detrimental," convey to the decisionmaker that the child in question is already a victim of his environmental circumstances, that he is greatly at risk, and that speedy action is necessary to avoid further harm being done to his chances of healthy psychological development. Secondly, the old guideline, in context and as construed by legislature, administrative agency, and court, has come to mean something less than what is in the child's best interests. The child's interests are often balanced against and frequently made subordinate to adult interests and rights. Moreover, and less forthrightly, many decisions are "in-name-only" for the best interests of the specific child who is being placed. They are fashioned primarily to meet the needs and wishes of competing adult claimants or to protect the general policies of a child care or other administrative agency.[1] But, even if the child's rights were, in fact and policy, determinative and thus unequivocally superior to adult interests,[2] the guideline would remain inadequate.

The tension between the apparent meaning of the best interest standard and its construction in legislative and court decision is illustrated by a case involving an infant boy named W.[3] The case highlights most of the problems with which we are concerned in this volume. These include the hazards of weighing the adults' interests against those of the child, of broken relationships, and of losing sight of the child's needs when there are adult claimants in conflict. This case also demonstrates the risks to the child of the delays that are a regular feature of the adult-centered court review and appeal. It also indicates how fragmented is the knowledge of child development that has entered and confused the thinking of courts and legislatures in their efforts to solve these problems of child placement. The ultimate outcome, however, reveals a court's capacity to construe with flexibility a legal doctrine in transition. But the tortured route by which the court reached the "right" result underlines the need for giving recognition to the new guideline and all of its component parts.

The case begins early in 1968, when an expectant mother arranged with the appropriate local authority for the adoption of her child at birth. As a consequence, the infant W was placed with "temporary" foster parents in March 1968. In September of the same year the foster parents decided that they wished to adopt W. Early in 1969 proceedings for adoption were initiated by the local authority and a hearing was scheduled for April. Meanwhile in March, the biological mother withdrew her consent—in accord with the Adoption Act which authorizes the withdrawal of the required consent at any time before an adoption order. The Act allows consent to be dispensed with only if the court is satisfied that the legal —usually biological—parent (a) has abandoned, neglected, or ill-treated the infant, or (b) is withholding consent *unreasonably*. Each of the three courts considering this case affirmed its commitment to abide by the priority of the Adoption Act, which makes the first and paramount consideration in placement through adoption the consent of the biological parent and second and subsidiary consideration the welfare of the child. Yet at the initial hearing in July of 1969 the county court judge focused on whether consent was being "unreasonably" withheld by the biological mother because of her failure to take into account the child's welfare. Sensitive to the child's need for continuity and despite the statutory subordination of the child's best interests, he changed the spirit of the statute, without altering its letter, and reversed the priorities:

> [I]nevitably it seems to me that to remove a child from the only home it has known and to put it in care of a stranger would, I think, not only disturb the child emotionally and cause untold tears and unhappiness and there might be a psychological disturbance as well. There is no medical evidence before me but it seems to me that one is entitled to take it into consideration as [pertaining to] the welfare of the child. [L]ooking at the matter quite dispassionately and saying what should a reasonable mother do in these circumstances—consent or refuse consent—I take the view, getting the guidance I can from the cases . . . that the reasonable mother should consent in all the circumstances of this case. . . . I feel she is unreasonably withholding consent in this case. I order that her consent should be dispensed with.[4]

In May of 1970 the county court judge's order of adoption was reviewed and reversed unanimously by the

Lords Justice of the Court of Appeal. Lord Justice Russell wrote:

> [I] cannot escape the conclusion that the judge's decision went entirely on his view as to the best interests of the child, nothwithstanding his self-reminder that on this point that was not the sole consideration.[5]

According to Lord Justice Cross,

> The task of the judge in deciding custody cases— and indirectly, therefore, in deciding contested adoption cases—has undoubtedly been made more difficult than it used to be by developments in medical thought over the past 20 years or so. Before the war it was, I think, generally assumed that although he might be made temporarily unhappy, a young child would not be lastingly disturbed by being transferred, even after a prolonged stay, from the care of foster parents or prospective adopters to his natural parents if both were approximately equally well-qualified to look after him. But nowadays speialists agree in saying that there is some risk of lasting emotional disturbance to any child who is removed from the care of one woman to that of another between the ages of six months and 2½ years. . . . But although the problem has been undoubtedly to some extent complicated by this development of medical opinion, I do not think that the complication affects this case.

Making crucial the biological mother's intent, not the impact on *W* of abandonment or the disruption of his relationship with his psychological parents, he added:

> I do not think that a mother who maintained her wish to retain her status as a mother in face of such general evidence would be considered to be acting unreasonably within the meaning of Paragraph 5 of the Act.[6]

Lord Justice Sachs, construing the Adoption Act most narrowly and forthrightly, observed:

> To resolve the contests between a parent and proposed adopters on the basis that normally the correct test is to take the course which is in the better general welfare interests of the child is plainly wrong. It ignores the necessity first to establish culpable conduct by the parent. To change to that test from the approach laid down by the Act could entail far-reaching and grievous consequences as against parents unwilling to forfeit their parenthood. It is, of course, . . . open to the legislature after considering those consequences to make such a change. It is not open to the courts, by adopting a 'welfare' approach to the [meaning of "withholding consent unreasonably"] to effect by a side wind a change contrary to the legislature's intentions.[7]

By April 1971, by just such a "side wind" as the Lords Justice would not effect, the House of Lords reinstated the adoption order. With apodictic assurance, Lord Hailsham disposed of the issue, but not of the ambiguity and the ambivalence which surrounds the doctrine:

> It is clear that the test is reasonableness and not anything else. It is not culpability. It is not indifference. It is not failure to discharge parental duties. It is reasonableness, and reasonableness in the context of the totality of the circumstances. But although welfare *per se* is not the test, the fact that a reasonable parent does pay regard to the welfare of his child must enter into the question of reasonableness as a relevant factor. It is relevant in all cases if and to the extent that a reasonable parent would take it into account. It is decisive in those cases where a reasonable parent must so regard it.

* * *

> This means that, in an adoption case, a county court judge applying the test of reasonableness must be entitled to come to his own conclusions, on the totality of the facts, and a revising court should only dispute his decision where it feels reasonably confident that he has erred in law, or acted without adequate evidence, or where it feels that his judgment of the witnesses and their demeanour has played so little part in his reasoning that the revising court is

in a position as good as that of the trial judge
to form an opinion. . . .

[I]t does not follow from the fact that the
test is reasonableness that any court is entitled
simply to substitute its own view for that of the
parent. In my opinion, it should be extremely
careful to guard against this error. Two reasonable parents can perfectly reasonably come to
opposite conclusions on the same set of facts
without forfeiting their title to be regarded as
reasonable. The question in any given case is
whether a parental veto comes within the band of
possible reasonable decisions and not whether it
is right or mistaken. Not every mistaken exercise
of judgment is unreasonable. There is a band of
decisions within which no court should seek to
replace the individual's judgment with his own.

*   *   *

Obviously, in a case without medical evidence it is necessary to be extremely careful in
assessing any possible danger to the child from
uprooting it from this stable and happy family
atmosphere and plunging it into the uncertainties
of (a new) menage. But, in my opinion, the
county court judge was well-entitled . . . to come
to the conclusion which he reached.[8]

Substantively, then, we could call the final decision not to alter *W*'s placement the least detrimental

alternative. And in two respects the procedure was in accord with that guideline. Consent for adoption, in accord with both the continuity and the child's-sense-of-time guidelines, was arranged by the local authority before W's birth. Further, during the process of review, and also in accord with the continuity guideline, W's relationship with his "foster-adopting" parents was uninterrupted. In contrast with many similar situations in the United States, W was not transferred to the biological mother following the intermediate appellate decision, only to be shunted back to the adopting parents months later in response to the decision by the House of Lords.

But the ultimate result and the positive features of the placement procedure should not obscure the detriments in the present system. Had the overall guideline we propose been adopted, the two and a half years of uncertainty which clouded the developing relationship with his adopting parents could have been avoided for W. If it were to follow the component guidelines of continuity and sense of time, a new Adoption Act would not authorize withdrawal of consent after a relationship with another adult had begun to develop—as it had in W's case. Such an Act would have required permanent placement of W as soon as consent was granted or as soon as possible thereafter.[9] Temporary placement with foster parents would have been allowed only if it had been the least detrimental alternative at the time. Our emphasis on the crucial role of a psychological parent would have given W the status of a wanted child. The county court judge, rather than having to pursue a roundabout course as he did, would have dismissed the action by the biological mother. He would have asserted that the law, in accord with a child's need for continuity, presumes in a case such as W's that the present, and now long-standing custody ought not to be disturbed.

The court would place the burden to overcome that presumption squarely on the adult claimant who challenges the existing relationship. To do otherwise would increase rather than minimize the detriments to the child.

Under the new Act, each child placement would be treated as a matter of urgency to be finally resolved in days not years.[10] Thus, to safeguard not only the child's needs but also the right of all adult claimants to a fair hearing and in order to minimize the pain of what may prove for them to be false hopes, W's case should have been treated as an emergency for all the parties concerned. Otherwise the process of review would afford the adult a hollow right and, more significantly, heighten the risk to the child. In sum, the case of W demonstrates the significance of altering the overall guideline governing child placement from the aim of doing good to the more modest aim of minimizing harm.

Whether the problem arises in separation, divorce, adoption, neglecting parent, foster care, or even juvenile delinquency proceedings,[11] the overall guideline for decision which we propose is to select "that placement which is the least detrimental among available alternatives for the child."* To use "detrimental" rather than

---

* A child whose placement must be determined in legal controversy has already been deprived of his "best interests," either by

"best interest" should enable legislatures, courts, and child care agencies to acknowledge and respond to the inherent detriments in any procedure for child placement as well as in each child placement decision itself. It should serve to remind decisionmakers that their task is to salvage as much as possible out of an unsatisfactory situation. It should reduce the likelihood of their becoming enmeshed in the hope and magic associated with "best," which often mistakenly leads them into believing that they have greater power for doing "good" than "bad."

The concept of "available alternatives" should press into focus how limited is the capacity of decisionmakers to make valid predictions and how limited are the choices generally open to them for helping a child in trouble. If the choice, as it may often be in separation and divorce proceedings, is between two psychological parents and if each parent is equally suitable in terms of the child's most immediate predictable developmental needs, the least detrimental standard would dictate a quick, final, and unconditional disposition to either of the competing parents.[12]

The proposed standard is less awesome and grandiose, more realistic, and thus more amenable to relevant data-gathering than "best interest." It should facilitate weighing the advantages and the disadvantages of the actual options. Yet, it too can be compromised and lita-

---

the loss of his parents; or by their rejection, ineptitude, and negligence; or by the breaking up of his family ties for other reasons. It it clearly beyond the court's power to undo the disturbances that have been caused in his development.

nized. But there is in any new formulation an opportunity, at least, for legislatures, courts, and agencies to reexamine their tasks and thus to perceive more easily factors of low visibility which have resulted in decisions actually against "the best interests of the child" as it has come to be understood and applied.

Chapter 5

On Party Status and the Right to Representation

THE CHILD IN ANY CONTESTED PLACEMENT SHOULD HAVE FULL PARTY STATUS AND THE RIGHT TO BE REPRESENTED BY COUNSEL *

Whether the overall guideline to child placement is in terms of best interest or least detrimental alternative, the court cannot do "complete justice" unless the child is recognized as a necessary, indeed, indispensable party to the proceeding.[1] Such a party is anyone who has a direct personal interest in the decision and whose rights might be adversely affected by it. Yet, despite the obvious stake each child has in his placement, courts and legislatures have failed to grant him party status, or to establish his right to representation by counsel, except in juvenile deliquency proceedings.[2]

The law presumes that a child's parents are generally best suited to represent and safeguard his inter-

* On the role of counsel in the child placement process see Chapter 7 in *Before the Best Interests of the Child* (Free Press, 1979).

ests.* That presumption, however, should not prevail, as it does, once the child's placement becomes the subject of a dispute between parents which they are unable to resolve without resort to the courts, as in a divorce or separation proceeding.⁴ That presumption should not prevail, as it does, when the state challenges their fitness to remain parents. Nor should it be presumed, as it is, that the state represents the interests of the child. Its policies or practices may conflict with those of the child. Nor should it be presumed, as it is, that a child is represented by each and all or any of the adult participants in a dispute between adopting, foster, or biological parents, or when such "parents" are in dispute with a child care agency. Even child care agencies which are delegated responsibility for safeguarding the welfare of children often have conflicts of interests between their need to safeguard some agency policy and the needs of the specific child to be placed. In none of these proceedings does anyone have a conflict-free interest in representing the child.

Crucial, then, to the informed implementation of the guidelines to child placement is not only party status for the child as a person in his own right but also adequate provision for his personal representation by counsel who has no other goal than to determine what is the least detrimental alternative for his client.⁵ In proceed-

---

* Of course, the needs of the individual family members do not automatically coincide with each other. Practical steps taken for the benefit of one are often at the same time not in the interest of another. Families vary according to preference being given either to the father's or the mother's or the children's concerns. However, so long as the family is held together by bonds of affection and mutual dependency, whatever arrangements are arrived at pay at least partial regard to all its members.³

ings before the court or administrative agency, counsel for the child must independently interpret and formulate his client's interests, including the need for a speedy and final determination.

In emphasizing the significance of party status and representation we do not intend to obscure another problem which must be acknowledged and which is beyond easy resolution. It is the problem of resistance by judges and other decisionmakers in law to our knowledge about child development which somehow does not fit their "commonsense" sense of the matter before them or, perhaps, threatens some private notion of what is "right" or "decent" or "moral." But party status and the right to representation may facilitate the exposure of such resistance and over time check its impact by adding one more potential appellant to the processes of review.

In sum, children, far from sharing the adults' concerns, are frequently put in direct conflict with them: their needs may contrast with those of their biological parents, their foster parents, or the social agencies concerned with them. For this reason, once their custody is questioned, their rights cannot be represented adequately by the advocates of either the adult claimant or the adult defendant. They need party status before any court or administrative agency concerned with their fate, namely, to be represented, independently of the adults, as persons in their own right.

A child's advocate must, of course, be sufficiently knowledgeable about children and their development to determine what information he must obtain and present about the specific child he represents. Our guidelines should facilitate his task.

Part Three

The Guidelines Applied

Chapter 6

The Rothman Decisions

We reproduce in full the actual decision about the placement of Stacey, an eight-year-old foster child, by Trial Justice Nadel of the New York Supreme Court. Following this, we rewrite his decision in accord with our overall guideline of the least detrimental alternative.

DECISION 1

> ROTHMAN V. JEWISH CHILD CARE ASSOCIATION
> Supreme Court New York County
> 166 *N.Y. Law Journal,* p. 17, Col. 1
> (Nov. 5, 1971)

JUSTICE NADEL

In this proceeding, the natural mother seeks a judgment for the return of her eight-year-old daughter, Stacey. Petitioner gave her daughter to respondents for temporary care in December, 1964, when she voluntarily entered a hospital

for treatment of a mental illness. Petitioner left
the hospital for a period of time and then was
readmitted. In December, 1969, the petitioner
was released from the hospital and has not been
hospitalized since. She is living with her parents,
is employed as an executive secretary, and earns
$140 per week.

The petitioner has never surrendered the
child for adoption. The respondent, Jewish Child
Care Association, opposes giving custody to the
natural mother on the ground that she is unfit
to care for the child by reason of her vast mental
illness. However, on the trial they failed to produce any evidence upon which the court could
make a finding that the petitioner is unfit to have
custody of the child. The burden is upon the nonparent respondent to prove that petitioner is
unfit to care for her daughter, and that the child's
well-being requires separation from her mother.
The Court of Appeals has ruled that absent abandonment of the child, statutory surrender of the
child or the established unfitness of the mother,
a court is without power to deprive the mother of
custody (*Spence-Chapin Adoption Service* v.
Polk, N.Y.L.J., Sept. 27, 1971, p. 1, col. 1). At
best, respondents have shown that the relationship between mother and daughter is not as good
as it should be. That this is so, is primarily the
fault of the Jewish Child Care Association. Its
extrajudicial determination that the child should
not be returned, its hindrance of visitation and

its failure to encourage the parental relationship were, to a great extent, responsible for the lack of a better relationship. It has been established in the Family Court that the said Association failed to make any real efforts to encourage and strengthen the parental relationship. The petitioner had to commence court proceedings for visitation and custody of her child, which were denied her by the Association.

Not only have respondents failed to sustain their burden of proof, but the evidence submitted amply demonstrates petitioner's fitness to have custody of her child. It was in the interest of the welfare of her daughter that the petitioner gave respondents temporary custody when she was hospitalized and unable to care for the child.

In the period of nearly two years preceding this trial, petitioner has been gainfully employed and she has been active in community, charitable and religious affairs. During the trying period of her hospitalization and separation from her child, petitioner appears to have successfully rehabilitated herself.

The court has observed petitioner during the course of her testimony. After hearing and observing the petitioner, the court finds that she is sincere in her desire to care for her daughter, and that she is able to do so. Petitioner is residing with her parents, and they will be able to care for their grandchild in the interim between the child's return from school and the time when the petitioner comes home from work. Their presence adds two persons to aid petitioner in the care of her daughter.

The request by the attorneys for the respondent Association to reargue the motion to refer this case to the Family Counseling Service is denied. Similar relief was denied respondent by several justices of this court. In any event, there has been a trial of the issues involved, and the courts finds no valid reason for any further delay in returning the child to her natural mother.

The petitioner indicated that she realizes that the attitude of her daughter may require a transitional period before acquiring full custody. The parties shall, therefore, confer and shall submit in the judgment to be settled herein, a program for visitation and transfer of custody. Should the parties fail to agree, the court will determine such provisions, giving due consideration to their suggestions.

Settle judgment. Exhibits are with the clerk of the part.

* * *

Judge Baltimore, a fictitious figure accepting our guidelines, rewrites Justice Nadel's opinion. In reaching his decision, he uses only the data relied upon by Justice Nadel. Beyond this, Judge Baltimore, in order to keep Stacey and her interests in focus, has, in restating the facts, refrained from using such emotionally freighted and conclusion-tending words and phrases as "natural mother" or "mother" in describing Ms. Rothman. He uses the words "petitioner" and "respondent" rather than continuously repeating the real names of the parties to the proceeding, and identifies Ms. Rothman only as an adult who gave birth to a female child named Stacey.

DECISION 1 REWRITTEN

ROTHMAN V. JEWISH CHILD CARE ASSOCIATION
Supreme Court Hampstead-Haven County
1 *New World Law Journal,* p. 1, Col. 1
(Nov. 5, 1971)

JUDGE BALTIMORE

In this proceeding, the petitioner, an adult woman, seeks our judgment to award to her for custody and care an eight-year-old female child named Stacey. To support her claim, she established the following uncontested facts:

1. In December of 1963 petitioner gave birth to Stacey and, in accord with custom, practice, and the law, was initially and automatically assigned parental responsibility for the custody and care of the infant.

2. Seven years ago petitioner entered the hospital for treatment of a mental illness. At the same time, she gave Stacey, then one year old, to the Jewish Child Care Association, the respondent, with the intention that she be cared for temporarily.

3. Two years ago, petitioner was released from

the hospital and has not been hospitalized since. She is now living with her parents, is employed as an executive secretary, and earns $140 per week.

4.   Petitioner is sincere in her request to care for Stacey, and her parents are prepared to assist in this while she is at work.

5.   The respondent has refused to disturb Stacey's present relationship with her adult custodians. It has hindered petitioner's efforts to visit Stacey and to establish a parental relationship.

The respondent, on Stacey's behalf, opposed giving custody to petitioner. Because of her prior illness, it asserts that she is unfit to care for the child, to serve as a parent. So far as this case is concerned, petitioner is, as is any other adult, initially presumed in law to be fit to be a parent. We need not and do not reach that question.

The real question is: does Stacey need to have a parent assigned to her by the court? The petitioner's fitness could have become an issue only had it first been established that Stacey is currently an unwanted child in need of a parent. Not until then could the court admit evidence concerning the petitioner in order to determine who, among the available alternatives, would serve Stacey's interests by providing the least detrimental opportunity for meeting her needs.

What is strangely missing from the evidence is any material evidence on Stacey's needs. In the absence of such evidence the law must and does presume that Stacey is a wanted child, well settled in a reciprocal relationship with her custodians. The burden is on the petitioner to overcome the presumption that the adult or adults who currently are responsible for Stacey are fit to remain her parents. Another facet of these presumptions is that Stacey has been psychologically abandoned by her biological mother. Seven years have elapsed since their last contact. The burden then is on petitioner to establish that there is a necessity for altering the long-standing ongoing relationship between Stacey and whoever may be her psychological parents. In short, petitioner must establish that Stacey is unwanted in her present family. If petitioner were to meet that burden, she would not then have to prove her fitness to be a parent. Rather, she would have to establish that among the available alternatives, her taking custody would be the least detrimental for Stacey's physical and psychological well-being.

Petitioner further argues that she never lost custody-in-law of Stacey. She established that she has always considered herself responsible for Stacey's care, that she had made "temporary" arrangements for her with the respondent, that from the outset it was understood that they were to be temporary, and that she had always intended, once her health was restored, to care personally for Stacey. At no time during the last seven years, she asserts, has she abandoned Stacey; has she ever ceased being her "mother." If anyone is at fault, it is, she claims, the respondent Association. It has prevented her from maintaining or, at least, establishing a parental relationship with Stacey.

These arguments and the supporting facts reflect

an understandable, but still mistaken notion. Abandonment of a child by an adult, at least for the purpose of determining who is parent, rests, not on the intentions of the adult, but rather on the impact such a leave-taking has on the child. Stacey, since the age of one year, has been deprived of continuous, affectionate, and otherwise nurturing contact with petitioner. In the absence of specific evidence to the contrary, for purposes of custody and care Stacey must be presumed in law to have been abandoned. If nothing else, from Stacey's vantage point, there has been a critical break in whatever psychological tie had begun to develop between herself and petitioner. Painful as it must be for this well-meaning woman, her intentions alone are not enough to prevent such psychological abandonment. Even if those intentions had been accompanied by a carefully designed program to maintain contact with the child, over the time elapsed petitioner could hardly have been the primary adult source for Stacey of affection, stimulation, and, most importantly, of a sense of continuity essential to securing healthy growth and development.

So far as Stacey's interests are concerned, it matters not that the implementation of those intentions may have actually been thwarted by the staff of the respondent Association or by anyone else, nor does it matter, for purposes of determining custody, whether petitioner's intentions were defeated through her misunderstanding, her illness, or her ignorance. Whatever the cause, whoever may feel responsible, the psychological fact, which the law must acknowledge, is that Stacey does not now recognize petitioner as a parent.

It would be impossible to locate precisely the moment in time when petitioner's "temporary" relinquishment of Stacey became abandonment. Nor is it possible to determine just when a new psychological parent-child relationship was formed. Nevertheless, in the absence of contrary evidence, it must be presumed that such a relationship developed over the past seven years. That relationship deserves the recognition and protection of the law, and may be perceived, not unlike common-law marriage, as common-law parenthood or common-law adoption. Such an adoption carries with it all the legal protections generally available to nurture and secure healthy ties between parent and child.[1]

This decision is not and must not be read to require the assigning of fault to any person or to any child placement agency.* Their intent is not relevant to the decision. By shifting the focus of decision to the problem of meeting the needs of the child, the law moves, as it should, away from making moral judgments about fitness to be a parent; away from assigning blame; and away from looking at the child and the award or denial of custody as reward or punishment. It becomes unimportant then whether the parent-child relationship grew out of circumstances within or beyond the "control" of an adult claimant.

Even if the Court decreed that Stacey be returned to her biological "mother," it would be wholly beyond its

---

* Of course, an agency may lose its license or be liable for damages if it is negligent in carrying out responsibilities it undertakes. What is important here is that the child not become the award for damages.

power to establish a psychological parent-child relationship between them. In addition, far from being benign, such a decree would inflict damage and pain on all parties, child as well as adults.

Though the status of parent is not easily lost in law, it can exist only so long as it is real in terms of the health and well-being of the child. It is a relationship from birth, whether legitimate or illegitimate, or from adoption, whether statutory or common-law, which requires a continuing interaction between adult and child to survive. It can be broken by the adult parent by "chance," by the establishment of a new adult-child relationship, which we call common-law adoption, or by "choice," through a more formal legal process we have come to call adoption. It is the real tie—the reality of an ongoing relationship—that is crucial to this court's decision and that demands the protection of the state through law. The court must not, despite its sympathetic concern for the petitioner, become a party to tearing Stacey away from the only affectionate parents she knows. Stacey must be presumed to be, in her present surroundings, a wanted child.

Finally, it must be observed that this decision does not constitute a break with the past. Rather, the past is future. There is in law, as psychoanalysis teaches that there is in man, a rich residue which each generation preserves from the past, modifies for the now, and in turn leaves for the future. Law is, after all, a continuous process for meeting society's need for stability by providing authority and precedent and, at the same time, meeting its need for flexibility and change by providing for each authority a counterauthority and for each precedent a counterprecedent. The living law thus seeks to secure an environment conducive to society's healthy growth and development.

That this decision is not incompatible with legal decisions of the last century will come as no surprise then, either to students of law who constructively resist sharp breaks with the past or to students of child development who have made us understand man's need for continuity. In 1824, for example, the distinguished American jurist and Justice of the United States Supreme Court, Joseph Story, had no psychoanalytic theory of child development to draw upon, yet, acting as circuit judge, he could write in *U.S.* v. *Green* (3 Mason 482 Fed. Cas. No. 15256 [1824]):

> As to the question of the right of the father to have the custody of his infant child, in a general sense it is true. But this is not on account of any absolute right of the father, but for the benefit of the infant, the law presuming it to be for its interests to be under the nurture and care of his natural protector, both for maintenance and education. When, therefore, the court is asked to lend its aid to put the infant into the custody of the father, and to withdraw him from other persons, it will look into all the circumstances, and ascertain whether it will be for the real, permanent interests of the infant and if the infant be of sufficient discretion, it will also consult its personal wishes.

Far less vague and in language often sounding psychoanalytic, yet written more than a decade before Freud published *The Interpretation of Dreams,* are the words of Justice Brewer speaking for the Supreme Court of Kansas in 1889 in the child placement case of *Chapsky* v. *Wood* (26 Kan. Reports, pp. 650–658 [2nd ed. annotated, 1889]):

> [When a] child has been left for years in the care and custody of others, who have discharged all the obligations of support and care which naturally rest upon the parent, then, whether the courts will enforce the father's right to the custody of the child, will depend mainly upon the question whether such custody will promote the welfare and interest of such child. This distinction must be recognized. If, immediately after [giving up the child] reclamation be sought, and the father is not what may be called an unfit person by reason of immorality, etc., the courts will pay little attention to any mere speculation as to the probability of benefit to the child by leaving or returning it. In other words, they will consider that the law of nature, which declares the strength of a father's love is more to be considered than any mere speculation whatever as to the advantages which possible wealth and social position might otherwise bestow. But, on the other hand, when reclamation is not sought until a lapse of years, when new ties have been formed and a certain current given to the child's life and

thought, much attention should be paid to the probabilities of a benefit to the child from the change. *It is an obvious fact that ties of blood weaken, and ties of companionship strengthen, by lapse of time; and the prosperity and welfare of the child depend on the number and strength of these ties, as well as on the ability to do all which the promptings of these ties compel* [our italics].

[T]hey who have for years filled the place of the parent, have discharged all the obligations of care and support, and especially when they have discharged these duties during those years of infancy when the burden is especially heavy, when the labor and care are of a kind whose value cannot be expressed in money—when all these labors have been performed and the child has bloomed into bright and happy girlhood, it is but fair and proper that their previous faithfulness, and the interest and affection which these labors have created in them, should be respected. Above all things, the paramount consideration is, what will promote the welfare of the child? These, I think, are about all the rules of law applicable to a case of this kind.

. . . What the future of the child will be is a question of probability. No one is wise enough to forecast or determine absolutely what would or what would not be best for it; yet we have to act upon these probabilities from the testimony before us, guided by the ordinary laws of human experience. . . .

[T]he child has had, and has today, all that a mother's love and care can give. The affection which a mother may have and does have, springing from the fact that a child is her offspring, is an affection which perhaps no other one can really possess; but so far as it is possible, springing from years of patient care of a little, helpless babe, from association, and as an outgrowth from those little cares and motherly attentions bestowed upon it, an affection for the child is seen in Mrs. Wood that can be found nowhere else. And it is apparent, that so far as a mother's love can be equaled, its foster-mother has that love, and will continue to have it.

On the other hand, if she goes to the house of her father's family, the female inmates are an aunt, just ripening into womanhood, and a grandmother; they have never seen the child; they have no affection for it springing from years of companionship. . . .

Human impulses are such that doubtless they would form an affection for the child—it is hardly possible to believe otherwise; but to that deep, strong, patient love which springs from either motherhood, or from a patient care during years of helpless babyhood, they will be strangers.

In acknowledging Stacey's adoption by affirming the respondent Association's assertion of the right to remain with her psychological parents of the past eight years, the court takes the position of Justice Brewer in the *Chapsky* case:

> It is a serious question, always to be considered, whether a change should be advised. "Let well enough alone" is an axiom founded on abundant experience [at p. 656].
> So ordered.

* * *

Almost one year after the Nadel and Baltimore opinions were written, Justice Nadel was asked to reconsider his first decision on the placement of Stacey. Here follows his second opinion in full, which invites comment.

DECISION 2

ROTHMAN V. JEWISH CHILD CARE ASSOCIATION
Supreme Court New York County
N.Y. Law Journal, p. 17, Col. 2–4
(Nov. 1, 1972)

JUSTICE NADEL

In this *habeas corpus* proceeding, brought by the mother against the Jewish Child Care Association, the court, after a hearing, directed the return of the then eight and one-half-year-old girl to her mother. The petitioner never surrendered the child for adoption, but had placed the child with respondents for temporary care in December, 1964, when she voluntarily entered a hospital for treatment of a mental ailment. Petitioner left the hospital and then was readmitted. In December, 1969, she was released from the hospital and since then has not been hospitalized. She lives with her parents and is gainfully employed. The court found that the respondents failed to sustain their burden of proof as to the unfitness of the mother to have custody of her child.

The mother realized that the antagonistic attitude of her daughter towards her required a transitional period before she regained full custody. The decision of the court provided for such transitional period.

In a collateral proceeding, affidavits of doctors and a medical report were submitted, based upon examination of the child subsequent to the custody hearing, which indicated that it would be detrimental to the child's mental health if she were turned over to the mother at the time. The court, on its own motion, modified the judgment of February 16, 1972, which directed the return of the child to the mother on a specific date, and by amended order and judgment dated March 2, 1972, ordered that the physical custody of the child be returned to respondent Jewish Child Care Association to enable said Agency to place the child in a facility operated by it, which would offer the specialized care and therapy which she needed, and where she would be examined by an impartial child psychiatrist, and thereafter hearings would be held at which all parties would submit competent medical proof on the issue of when and under what circumstances the said child may be returned to the mother. The hearings were scheduled for June.

However, Chapters 645 and 646 of the Laws of 1972, effective May 30, 1972, added a provision to section 383, subdivision 3 of the Social Services Law, which was tailored to specifically fit the case at bar. It provided that foster parents having had continuous care of a child for more than twenty-four months through an authorized agency, shall be permitted as a matter of right, as an interested party to intervene in any proceeding involving the custody of the child. A motion made by the foster parents to intervene in this proceeding was granted by another Justice of this court by order dated June 27, 1972. This court had denied a motion seeking similar relief on March 1, 1972, prior to enactment of Chapters 645 and 646 of Laws of 1972, under authority of Scarpetta v. Spence-Chapin Adoption Service, 28 N. Y. 2d 185. In order to afford the intervenors an opportunity to have their psychiatrist examine the child and then participate in the hearings, it was agreed to postpone the hearings to September.

The impartial psychiatrist Dr. D'Arc was selected by counsel for the petitioner and counsel for respondents from a panel submitted by the

President of the Council of Child Psychology.[2] Each of the parties, including the intervenors, had an opportunity to examine the child by a psychiatrist of its own choosing. Dr. D'Arc examined the child on four separate occasions.

Five psychiatrists have testified and they are unanimous in their opinion that the child is depressed and that the mere mention of the possibility of returning her to the natural mother evokes depression, sadness and tears. It is significant that not even Dr. Cohen, the psychiatrist called by the petitioner, recommends that the child be returned to her natural mother. To do so would be detrimental to the child's well-being.

Dr. Cohen felt that if the child must be turned over to the mother it should be done in a gradual way so that there would not be any undue pressure on either of the participants. He suggested a plan whereby initially the visits by the mother would be at Pleasantville for an hour or two at a time to develop a rapport, then for several hours to visit local places, and if this proceeded well, then perhaps for a day at the mother's home, and if this worked well, then for periods of a weekend, and if this plan continued to work well, for periods of a week or longer.

This plan is somewhat similar to the gradual transition recommended originally by this court. The record indicates that the visits pursuant to the court's recommended gradual transition did not work out well in its initial stages, and that the visits in Pleasantville during July through September were a complete failure.

In answer to the question, "What if the visits do not proceed well?" Dr. Cohen stated:

"Well, what I'm saying, I guess, is this: that if visits would not work out on a regular basis well, if there was a consistent pattern of total lack of rapport, if there was no progress being made, then certainly one would have to question whether that will work out."

And in answer to the question, "Assuming the initial visits at Pleasantville did not work out okay?" he stated:

"Well, I think if the initial visits did not work out all right and one was not able to determine what was it that might be interfering with them working out, then it might indeed be that further visits would not be in order."

He also testified that the child had adverse feelings to the possibility of being united with her mother, that she felt dejected, upset and tearful.

Dr. Feldman and Dr. Damino, the psychiatrists called by the intervenors, indicated that the child was depressed and was likely to develop some very dangerous propensities if forced to return to her mother. They felt strongly that the child should not be returned to the mother at the present time. Dr. Damino testified that he had a plan whereby she could possibly develop a pleasant relationship with her child. He stated:

"I concluded, from examination of the girl, that there is one probable way, and this is my opinion, and that is that if the natural mother is not a threat to the girl for several years, which I would estimate to be about—I'd say about five years, in my opinion, that if the natural mother is not a threat to the girl in regard to taking away the girl from the D.'s, then there is a substantial probability that the girl could develop some affectionate relationship to the natural mother if, seeing the natural mother, say on a regular basis, every two weeks for a day or two, but the main thing there would be that the natural mother would not be a threat to taking the girl away from the D.'s."

He further testified that at the present time there is no reliable possibility that Stacey can be returned to her mother without being a destroyed human being.

Dr. Pelner, called by the respondents, testified that the return of the child to the mother would result in mental deterioration of the child. He also testified that it was conceivable that some time in the distant future Stacey may want to consider being returned to her mother, perhaps even being curious of her mother and wanting to establish some contact with her. On cross-examination he stated that the quickest and surest way "for a child like Stacey to be able to reach the point, to reach out to her mother, I think would be actually via the D.'s."

Mr. Arest, the Resident Unit Administrator at Pleasantville Cottage School, testified as to the complete failure of the petitioner to establish any kind of rapport with the child on any of the visits. Although he made several efforts to help her during these visits, it was to no avail. The child came back after these visits crying hysterically, was very upset, was shaking. The child rejected all offers of affection by the mother. The mother then became frustrated, yelled at the child and threatened her. The visits were short and always ended on an unpleasant note; uncontradicted evidence is that the hostility of the child towards the mother has persisted, that the mother overreacted to the unyielding attitude of the child and could not win her affection or trust. The mother felt frustrated with her child. From all the testimony the court concludes that it would be against the best interests of the child and it would be detrimental and dangerous to the child's mental and emotional well-being to return her to the petitioner at this time.

The petitioner contends that since the court has heretofore found that the petitioner is not an unfit mother, the court is without option and must return Stacey forthwith because without a finding of unfitness the court cannot consider the child's well-being and cites as authority (People ex rel. Kropp v. Shepsky, 305 N. Y. 465; People ex rel. Scarpetta v. Spence-Chapin Adoption Service, 28 N. Y. 2d 185, 321 N. Y. S. 2d 65;

Spence-Chapin Adoption Service v. Polk, 29 N. Y. 2d 196, 324 N. Y. S. 2d 937).

This court does not believe that these cases hold absent a finding of unfitness of the mother, consideration of the child's well-being is prohibited, and the child must be ordered returned forthwith to the mother.

In Spence-Chapin Adoption Service v. Polk (supra), the Court of Appeals reviews the leading cases on the subject, reaffirms that the primacy of parental rights may not be ignored and that a contest between a parent and a nonparent may not resolve itself into a simple factual issue as to who can provide or afford the better surroundings or as to which party is better equipped to raise the child. Then the court states, at page 204:

" 'In other words, the burden rests, not, for instance, upon the mother to show that the child's welfare would be advanced by being returned to her. But rather upon the nonparents to prove that the mother is unfit to have her child and that the latter's wellbeing requires its separation from its mother.' (305 N.Y. at 469). Of course, this does not mean the child's rights and interests are subordinated. The principle rests on the generally accepted view that a child's best interest is that it be raised by its parent unless the parent is disqualified by gross misconduct. That the generalization has myriads of exceptions is equally true, but the exceptions do not contradict the verity of the principle."

Although the court repeats the language of the *Shepsky* case, supra, that the non-parents have the burden of proving "that the mother is unfit to have her child *and* that the latter's well-being required a separation from its mother" (emphasis ours), it immediately follows with qualifications (1) that the child's rights and interests are not subordinated and (2) that the generalization has myriads of exceptions.

General principles by themselves are not the only guide to action in specific cases. Sometimes the exceptions prove the rule. In none of the cases cited by the petitioner is there competent medical evidence that the transfer of custody to the mother would endanger the well-being of the child.

If the court failed to consider the child's mental and emotional well-being in this case it would indeed constitute a subordination of the child's rights and interests. The child is now a nine and one-half year old girl. The tragic experience during the first two years of her life, the continued absence of the mother during the next six and one-half years, the persistent rejection of the mother by the child during the past year, the mother's inability to develop any rapport or to cope with the child, regardless of who was at fault, and the comprehensive medical testimony that the child's mental and emotional well-being

would be endangered, warrant a finding that this
case comes within the myriads of exceptions to
the general principles of the primacy of parental
custody.

On the evidence, the court concludes that
to return the child to the mother at this time
would endanger the child's mental and emotional
well-being, and would be against the best interests of the child. The petition is therefore dismissed.

Settle judgment, providing for visitation
as discussed at conference with attorneys.

* * *

DECISION 2 EVALUATED

In contrast to Justice Nadel, our fictitious Judge Baltimore was spared the necessity to reverse his order on the
placement of Stacey. Neither did he need to treat her
case as one of the exceptions and to rely on medical evidence to justify his decision not to return her to her
biological mother. On the basis of knowledge extrapolated
from our guidelines, he was prepared for Stacey to be
firmly tied to the adults who had become her psychological parents, and to answer with dismay to any intrusion into this relationship.

In accord with our guideline on continuity, he
would have refrained from placing Stacey in temporary
surroundings, even if the biological mother had overcome
the presumption that the child was wanted and well

settled in her foster home. He would have left her there until alternative permanent placement (the least detrimental alternative) had been found.

In accord with our guideline on the child's sense of time, he would not have expected any attachment to the biological mother left in Stacey after seven years of separation, even though petitioner had been the child's first caretaker, and even though a psychological relationship may have begun to develop between them at that time.

Presuming that Stacey was a healthy child before the interference with her fate, he would have put less trust in the efficacy of "therapy" for her. A child's attachment to his psychological parent is normal and therefore not subject to therapeutic efforts which are designed to affect pathological manifestations. Stacey cannot be "cured" of her love for her foster parents.

In accord with the principle of making the child's interests paramount, he would not have accorded visitation rights to the biological mother since the child rejected her and therefore was unlikely to profit from her presence or influence. He would at the same time be protecting the rights and interests of the psychological parents.

Certainly, he would have wondered why there was not a clear statement that Stacey had been returned to the D.'s, and in view of his understanding of child development, why the psychiatric experts had accepted the initial effort to remove Stacey from her psychological parents. He also would have wondered if the first decision could ever have been made if Stacey had been accorded party status with adequate representation of her interests.*

* Stacey was adopted by her foster parents on March 1, 1974.

Chapter 7

Provisions for a Child Placement Statute

Here we present some of the basic ingredients for a child placement code.* Statutory provisions have been drafted to codify the concepts, guidelines, and conclusions of this volume. We do not provide the customary commentary for the code because the volume itself serves that function.[1]

SELECTED PROVISIONS FOR THE CHILD PLACEMENT CODE OF HAMPSTEAD-HAVEN

ARTICLE 10.   DEFINITIONS

PARA. 10.1   BIOLOGICAL PARENTS

The biological parents are those who physically produce the child.

---

* Additional provisions for a code are suggested in Appendix II of *Before the Best Interests of the Child* (Free Press, 1979).

PARA. 10.2   WANTED CHILD

A wanted child is one who receives affection and nourishment on a continuing basis from at least one adult and who feels that he or she is and continues to be valued by those who take care of him or her.

PARA. 10.3   PSYCHOLOGICAL PARENT

A psychological parent is one who, on a continuing, day-to-day basis, through interaction, companionship, interplay, and mutuality, fulfills the child's psychological needs for a parent, as well as the child's physical needs. The psychological parent may be a biological (Para. 10.1), adoptive, foster, or common-law (Para. 10.4) parent, or any other person. There is no presumption in favor of any of these after the initial assignment at birth (Para. 20).

PARA. 10.4   COMMON-LAW PARENT-CHILD RELATIONSHIP

A common-law parent-child relationship is a psychological parent (Para. 10.3)–wanted child (Para. 10.2) relationship which developed outside of adoption, assignment by custody in separation or divorce proceedings, or the initial assignment at birth of a child to his or her biological parents (Para. 20.1).

PARA. 10.5   CHILD'S SENSE OF TIME

A child's sense of time is based on the urgency of his or her instinctual and emotional needs and thus differs from an adult's sense of time, as adults are better able to anticipate the future and thus to manage delay. A child's sense of time changes as he or she develops. Intervals of separation between parent and child that would constitute important breaks in continuity at one age might be of reduced significance at a later age.

PARA. 10.6   LEAST DETRIMENTAL AVAILABLE ALTERNATIVE

The least detrimental available alternative is that child placement and procedure for child placement which maximizes, in accord with the child's sense of time (Para. 10.5), the child's opportunity for being wanted (Para. 10.2) and for maintaining on a continuous, unconditional, and permanent basis a relationship with at least one adult who is or will become the child's psychological parent (Para. 10.3).

ARTICLE 20.   INITIAL PLACEMENT

PARA. 20   PLACEMENT OF CHILD

At birth, a child is placed with his biological parents (Para. 10.1). Unless other adults assume or are assigned the role, they are presumed to become the child's psychological parents (Para. 10.3).

ARTICLE 30.   INTERVENTION TO ALTER A CHILD'S PLACEMENT

PARA. 30.1   STATE POLICY OF MINIMIZING DISRUPTION

It is the policy of this state to minimize disruptions of continuing relationships between a psychological parent (Para. 10.3) and the child. The child's developmental needs are best served by continuing unconditional and permanent relationships. The importance of a relationship's duration and the significance of a disruption's duration vary with the child's developmental stage.

PARA. 30.2 INTERVENOR

An intervenor is any person (including the state, institutions of the state, biological parents, and others) who seeks to disrupt a continuing relationship between psychological parent (Para. 10.3) and child or seeks to establish an opportunity for such a relationship to develop. Upon such interventions the court's decision must secure for the child the least detrimental available alternative (Para. 10.6).

PARA. 30.3 BURDEN ON THE INTERVENOR

A child is presumed to be wanted (Para. 10.2) in his or her current placement. If the child's placement is to be altered, the intervenor, except in custody disputes in divorce or separation, must establish *both*:

(i) that the child is unwanted, *and*

(ii) that the child's current placement is not the least detrimental available alternative (Para. 10.6).

In custody disputes in divorce or separation, the intervenor, that is the adult seeking custody, must establish that he or she is the least detrimental available alternative (Para. 10.6).

PARA. 30.4 CHILD'S PARTY STATUS

Whenever an intervenor seeks to alter a child's placement the child shall be made a party to the dispute. The child shall be represented by independent counsel.*

---

* See Chapter 7 of *Before the Best Interests of the Child* (Free Press, 1979).

PARA. 30.5   FINAL UNCONDITIONAL DISPOSAL

All placements shall be unconditional and final, that is, the court shall not retain continuing jurisdiction over a parent-child relationship or establish or enforce such conditions as rights of visitation.*

PARA. 30.6   TIMELY HEARING AND APPEAL

Trials and appeals shall be conducted as rapidly as is consistent with responsible decisionmaking. The court shall establish a timetable for hearing, decision, and review on appeal which, in accord with the specific child's sense of time (Para. 10.5), shall maximize the chances of all interested parties to have their substantive claims heard while still viable, and shall minimize the disruption of parent-child relationships (Para. 30.1).

* See Epilogue.

Part Four

Examining Our Premises

Chapter 8

Why Should the Child's Interests Be Paramount?

Some will assert that the views presented in this volume are so child-oriented as to neglect the needs and rights of the adults. In fact, this is not the case. There is nothing one-sided about our position, that the child's interests should be the paramount consideration once, but not before, a child's placement becomes the subject of official controversy. Its other side is that the law, to accord with the continuity guideline, must safeguard the rights of any adults, serving as parents, to raise their children as they see fit, free of intervention by the state, and free of law-aided and law-abetted harassment by disappointed adult claimants.* To say that a child's ongoing relationship with a specific adult, the psychological parent, must

* Of course, all parents are subject to state intervention for delinquency, neglect, abandonment, and child abuse. This observation does not imply that the law has developed adequate standards for making such findings.[1]

not be interrupted, is also to say that this adult's rights
are protected against intrusion by the state on behalf of
other adults.

As set out in this volume, then, a child's placement should rest entirely on consideration for the child's
own inner situation and developmental needs. Simple as
this rule sounds, there are circumstances which make it
difficult to apply even with ample evidence in support of
the child's interests. The injunction disregards that laws
are made by adults for the protection of adult rights.[2]

Adults have deeply engrained irrational reservations about the primacy of children's needs. These reservations—ambivalent feelings—cannot be guarded against
except by clear and compelling priorities once there is
conflict about the child's placement. The adult's negative
feelings may be limited, but not avoided, by their rational and affectionate regard for children.* Once the
child is the focus of conflict between adults or their institutions, there are an infinite number of disguised ways in
which these irrational negative attitudes will find expression. Such negative attitudes are adult reactions to
the demands, competitive tendencies, and regressive influences of the child. Additionally, and most basically,
these destructive attitudes express the parents' expectant
sense that they will be replaced by the child. Adults
universally experience children as representatives of their
mortality as well as their immortality.

Court decisions are made by judges who, like
other human beings, tend to hold people responsible for

---

* Similarly, the adult's positive, affectionate feelings, if not
sufficiently tempered, impose an undue burden on the child.

the consequences of their own willful actions or to sympathize with them when actions are forced upon them, against their will, by adversities beyond their control.

Judges may be ready to be convinced by the arguments of the child's counsel and find against a biological parent who claims possession of a child whom he has deliberately abandoned in the first instance, or concerning whose adoption he has changed his mind belatedly. Many might argue that, after all, the claimant's loss of the child is the logical result of his own behavior.

Where abandonment by the biological parent is wholly involuntary, the judge, notwithstanding the child's need, may respond entirely differently. He will judge the parents as innocent victims of war, illness, or any other form of *force majeure*. An outstanding example are the Jewish parents of Holland who returned from concentration camps to reclaim their children at the close of the Second World War. They had entrusted their children to non-Jewish compatriots and were looking forward to reunion. Many of these children had become totally estranged from their biological parents and had grown intimately into the families of their foster parents. The choice in such tragic instances is between causing intolerable hardship to the child who is torn away from his psychological parents, or causing further intolerable hardship to already victimized adults who, after losing freedom, livelihood, and worldly possessions may now also lose possession of their child.

In this case, the Dutch government decreed that the children would be returned to their biological parents, thereby not leaving the outcome to case-by-case determination by the courts.* Nevertheless, there are many situations of similar impact, no less tragic, though with less world appeal, confronting the decisionmakers in contested child placements. The guidelines clarify for such decisionmakers the range, complexity, and nature of the choices that confront them.

Judge Baltimore, usually an unwavering supporter of the child's interests, reveals how difficult and painful the choice is in the following decision.

> Despite my sympathetic concern for adults faced with tragedy, the choice before the court is no different, though apparently more difficult, than it often seems in foster parent-common-law adoption cases. Whatever the court decides, inevitably there will be hardship. It may be the biological parents, already victimized by poverty, poor education, ill health, prejudice, their own ambivalence, or other circumstances, who are denied their child. It may be the child who is torn away from his psychological parents. It may be the psychological parents who are deprived of the

* "At the end of the war some 4500 Jewish children were in hiding in this country. As regards about 2500 of them one parent or both parents survived the war and in these cases the children concerned were returned to their parents, as was prescribed by law.

"As regards the remaining 2000: most of them were entrusted to members of their Jewish families, but some 360 were left in the care of non-Jewish foster-parents and these cases led to violent disagreements, some of which were protracted over many years.

"There were therefore no conflicts 'between the two sets of parents.' Of course, there were emotional difficulties when the children were returned to their natural parents."[3]

child for whom they have long and faithfully cared. It may be all of them.

If I, in accord with my oath, am to implement the state's preference for serving the child's interests, my choice and decision are clear, though not, as they seldom are, easy. I must decide not to disturb the child's relationship with his common-law parents. More precisely, I must even deny the biological parents an opportunity to call into question the existing placement of "their" child unless they could introduce evidence that "their" child is neglected or abandoned. Harsh as it is and as it must seem to the biological parents, their standing in court is no greater than that of a stranger.

As a judge, I have to recognize as irrelevant feelings which have been aroused in me because of my childhood experiences, my own concerns about being a parent, and my religious origins. These feelings would compel me to place the child with the biological parents, as compensation for their suffering, were it not for the guideline which stresses the child's need for continuity.

Further, to return to the problem of judicial choice as originally posed, I maintain that, once the least detrimental alternative is found, such decisions maximize known benefit and minimize known harm for all parties concerned. To leave undisturbed the relationship of the child to his common-law parents protects the well-being of the largest number. To favor the biological parents would impose an intolerable hardship on both the child and the psychological parents. To favor the child would be to favor as well his psychological parents. If each human being's interest is entitled to equal weight, more interests will tilt the scale toward leaving well enough alone than toward allowing the biological parents to prevail.

Arguments have been made that the winning adult will suffer guilt for depriving the other adult of the child or that the child himself will feel let down by one set of parents or the other. But to attribute to the judicial process the capacity to work out and to weigh the significance of such imponderables in its decisionmaking is unrealistic.

Let me now address those who argue that the adults' interest, not the child's, should be paramount. Even if such a policy were adopted, the court would be hard pressed in most cases to determine whether the biological or the psychological parent or who of the divorcing parents would be most harmed by the denial of custody.

The state may, of course, assert another policy to be applied to cases of extreme hardship, resulting from major disasters approximating the Dutch situation. Parents who have been forced to relinquish their children against their wishes would have a primary and overriding right to regain their custody. The state would be committed to assist such parents in the search for their children and in enforcing their right to repossess them. It might be argued that any other policy would violate a fundamental ethic of a civilized society, regardless of the individual child's needs and state of mind.

But after reviewing the arguments for each of these policies, I return to the guidelines that have governed my decisions. I am convinced that, by and large, society must use each child's placement as an occasion for protecting future generations of children by increasing the number of adults-to-be who are likely to be adequate parents. Only in the implementation of this policy does there lie a real opportunity for beginning to break the cycle of sickness and hardship bequeathed from one generation to the next by adults who as children were denied the least detrimental alternative.

Epilogue

Further Observations on the Application of the Least Detrimental Alternative Standard

Following its publication in 1973 this book provoked the critical comment of many persons concerned with children and the law. Here we address two of the issues which repeatedly attracted our attention and which suggested the need for clarification of the least detrimental alternative standard, particularly as it applies to disposition decisions.[1]

I. THE GUIDELINES—SIMPLICITY IS THE ULTIMATE SOPHISTICATION

Judge Nanette Dembitz of the Family Court of New York State is one of the most articulate expounders of the argument that the guidelines in *Beyond the Best Interests of the Child* oversimplify the complex issues in child placement disputes. In a review entitled "Beyond Any Discipline's Competence," she writes that the promise of the book to provide guidelines "is seductive but impossible; the authors fail to devise usable scales because the amalgams of factors to be appraised in custody contests are too complex." [2] Too complex for what? Surely not too complex to permit the court to decide what it cannot avoid deciding, namely, who among the competing adults or child care agencies is to prevail, who is to assume parental control and responsibility for the child. There is, however, an important truth in the title to the review. That truth, which judges often ignore, is that it is beyond the competence of any judge, or for that matter of any discipline, to appraise the amalgam of human factors in any child placement dispute for purposes of making long-term predictions or dictating special conditions for custody.

Those judges who share the Dembitz position confuse their *authority* to do with their *capacity* to do. They fail to realize that the *who* and *how* of custody are and must be separate. It is the *who* which judges must and can decide. It is the *how* which is beyond any judge's competence. But judges often fail to see what must be obvious once said, that the intricate and delicate character of the parent-child relationship places it beyond their constructive (though not beyond their destructive) reach.

Familial bonding is too complex and too vulnerable a process to be managed in advance or from a distance by so gross and impersonal an instrument as the law. In rejecting this simple guideline as simplistic, judges become the oversimplifiers. They seduce themselves into believing that they can penetrate the blindfolds of justice to weigh and to assess the "amalgams of factors" which are beyond the competence of all other disciplines.

Were judges to follow guidelines set forth in this book, they would restrict their activity to answering the one question that they really can and must answer, which is *who* shall have custody and not *how* or *under what conditions* the custodian and child are to relate to one another and to others. But, like the well-intentioned, overprotective, and often destructive parent who doesn't know when to let go, such judges decide not only *who* is to be parent, but also *how* the child is to be parented—for example, educated, medicated, and visited.

Too frequently judges behave as if the function of placement decisions is to provide a child with autonomous judges, not autonomous parents. They act as if the *parens patriae* doctrine and the best interests standard granted them the competence to be good, albeit absentee, super-parents with a veto power. Courts, administrative agencies, and the experts upon whom they rely must learn to reject such simplistic notions about parent-child relationships. They can no longer deny what their own experience should make obvious to them, which is that they have the time and capacity to damage but not to nurture or manage the healthy growth of familial bonds. In their professional roles they cannot be parent to someone else's children. At best and at most, law can provide a new opportunity for the relationship between a child and an adult to unfold free of coercive meddling by the state.

The psychoanalytically informed guidelines of continuity, of a child's sense of time, and of the limitations of law and knowledge are simple but not simplistic. They grew out of a recognition of how complex and vulnerable is the process of growing up. They recognize how vital it is to a child to be secure in the feeling that his "parents" are in charge and in control. Except for institutional placements and for temporary (truly short-term) foster care, judges must pull out decisively after deciding who shall have custody, in the expectation that the adults selected can be relied upon to meet their child's ever-changing day-to-day needs.[3] Precisely because human relationships are complicated, courts and administrative agencies must have simple guidelines which will lead to an immediate and unequivocal restoration of family privacy as each child is placed. No less is required by the presumptions of parental autonomy and a policy of minimum state intervention. Simplicity is the ultimate sophistication in deciding a child's placement.

II. VISITATION

Our conclusion that noncustodial parents should have "no legally enforceable right to visit" their children has proved to be the most misunderstood, most controversial, and most resisted aspect of our suggestion that all but emergency and other truly temporary placements should be unconditional. It has been misread to mean that we oppose the continuation of contact between a child and his noncustodial parent. It has been challenged with the argument that our position (a) conflicts with the least detrimental alternative standard, especially with the continuity guideline; (b) deprives a child of his basic right to maintain his ties to the noncustodial parent; and (c) places an instrument of revenge in the hands of the custodial parent (usually pictured as an angry mother) who will use it to spite the noncustodial parent (usually pictured as a thwarted and well-motivated father).[4]

We reasoned, always from the child's point of view, that custodial parents, not courts or noncustodial parents, should retain the right to determine when and if it is desirable to arrange visits.[5] We took and continue to take this position because it is beyond the capacity of courts to help a child to forge or maintain positive relationships to two people who are at cross-purposes with each other; because, by forcing visits, courts are more likely to prevent the child from developing a reliable tie to either parent; and because children who are shaken, disoriented, and confused by the breakup of their family need an opportunity to settle down in the privacy of their reorganized family with one person in authority upon whom they can rely for answers to their questions and for protection from external interference. After all, the goal of every placement decision, whether made at birth by certificate or later by more direct state intervention, is to provide each child with an opportunity—unbroken by further intrusion—to establish or reestablish and maintain psychological bonds to those to whom he is entrusted.*

A child develops best if he can have complete trust that the adults who are responsible for him are the arbiters of his care and control as he moves toward the

* Temporary placements should be subject to conditions in furtherance of this goal.[6] Short-term foster care and emergency placements should be designed and administered to safeguard and maintain the continuity of ties to absent parents with whom the child is expected to be reunited. And temporary placements pending final disposition in a custody dispute must assure that both competing adults have access to the child.

full independence of adulthood and gradually comes to
rely upon himself as his own caretaker. A court under-
mines that trust when it subjects his custodial parent to
special rules about raising him, for example, by ordering
(even scheduling) visits with the noncustodial parent.[7] In
the child's eyes, the court, by directing him to act against
the express wishes of his custodial parent, casts doubt
on that parent's authority and capacity to parent. It
damages, particularly for the younger child, his confidence
in his parent's power to shield him from unwanted and
painful threats from the outside. It invites the older
child to manipulate his parents by invoking the higher
authority of the court rather than to learn to work things
out with his custodial parent. We formulated the continuity guideline in direct response to such considerations.
We urged, therefore, that the already handicapped relationship between child and custodial parent not be
plagued by the never-ending threat of disruption by the
impersonal authority of the court.

However, we did not and do not oppose visits. Indeed, other things being equal, courts, in order to accord
with the continuity guideline, could award custody to
the parent who is most willing to provide opportunities
for the child to see the other parent. And—even though
we do not believe that a noncustodial father (or mother)
can play the same significant role in a child's life as a
parent in an intact family—we usually encourage custodial parents who seek our advice to facilitate the main-
tenance of the relationship between the child, particularly
the older child, and his noncustodial parent.* But such

* Visits under favorable circumstances are, at best, a poor
substitute for a parent in the family. Weekend visits do not com-

advice can and should be nothing more. Custodial parents must remain free to accept or reject our notions about the importance of continuity. The guideline cannot be pressed any further in favor of the child's now secondary relationship with the noncustodial parent without violating the child's need for continuity of the primary relationship to his custodial parent. As time goes by and as circumstances change, the child needs a parent who can work out with him ways of resolving his wishes to see and not to see the other parent as well as of dealing with his joys and sorrows following visits and his hurts when noncustodial parents refuse to maintain contact or fail to show. Meaningful visits for the child can occur only if both the custodial and the noncustodial parents are of a mind to make them work.[8] If so, a court order is both unnecessary and undesirable. If not, such orders and the threat or actual attempt to enforce them can do the child no good.[9]

Our reasons for objecting to court-enforceable visits seem to be recognized when courts resolve disputes about visitation that are camouflaged under the labels of "joint" or "split" custody. For example, in *Braiman* v.

---

pensate the child for parental absence at crucial moments in his life. Prolonged visits in the summer vacation only too often arouse unwillingness to return to the custodial parent or, at least, increase the loyalty conflict between the two "partners." But, once a child is past the age of five or six, he may be unwilling to give up the relationship to a parent who has played a large part in his early development. By that time he has outgrown his earlier unquestioning trust in parents, he has learned to criticize, to take sides in quarrels, to begin to understand that parents in some way share responsibility for the separation. In short, the progress in his cognitive capacity may help him with his emotional difficulties inherent in the situation.

Braiman Chief Judge Breitel of the New York Court of Appeals reversed a joint custody order for reasons that apply to all other types of visitation orders. The lower court had "awarded to the parents jointly [two sons aged six and seven and a half] to spend weekdays with the mother and weekends with the father." Judge Breitel said: "Entrusting the custody of young children to their [divorced] parents jointly, especially where the shared responsibility and control includes alternating physical custody, is insupportable when parents are severely antagonistic and embattled. . . . [I]t can only enhance family chaos. . . . It would, moreover, take more than reasonable self restraint to shield the children as they go from house to house, from the ill feelings, hatred, and disrespect each parent harbors towards the other.[10] After observing that the court must "recognize the division in fact of the family" and that "there are no painless solutions," Judge Breitel said: "In the rare case, joint custody may approximate the former family relationships more closely than other custodial arrangements. It may not, however, be indiscriminately substituted for an award of sole custody to one parent." [11] What the court fails to recognize is that no parent has sole custody so long as he or she is subject to rules of visitation, and that courts are as powerless to forge affection by a visitation order as they are by decreeing any other form of "joint," "divided," or "split" custody.*

Finally, courts and commentators, blinded by the

---

* Understandably, these terms are often used to describe the same arrangements. From a child's point of view, custody is likely to be "split" or "divided" rather than "joint" so long as his parents are in conflict.[12]

specter of spiteful custodial parents denying visits at the child's expense, have rejected our position with the misleading assertion that visitation or access is a right of the child, not of the parents. In fact, by subjecting an award of custody to an order imposing visits, the court does not protect the child's "basic right" to see his noncustodial parent.[13] It merely shifts the power to deprive the child of his "right" *from* the custodial parent *to* the noncustodial parent. Visitation orders make the noncustodial parent—rather than the parent who is responsible for the child's day-to-day care—the final authority for deciding if and when to visit. Even if the court orders visits because it believes they will serve the child's best interest, the noncustodial parent remains free not to visit, to "reverse" the court without risk of being in contempt. The court is powerless, as it should be, to order noncustodial parents to visit their "waiting" children. But the court has the corrosive power to have a child forcibly removed from a custodial parent who refuses to allow visits, or to imprison that parent for contempt. When it exercises such power, the court establishes for the child—and indeed for other children in the family who are not themselves subject to visitation orders—that his custodial parent cannot be trusted and is powerless to protect him. Courts obscure the real issues when they say what they cannot mean—that visitation is "a basic right of the child rather than a basic right of the parent." [14]

The reasoning and the consequences of an opinion by a New York Family Court Judge dramatically illustrate how courts justify the exercise of their power to force visits and why we continue to urge that they should be denied such authority:

PIERCE V. YERKOVICH
363 N.Y.S.2d 403 (1974)

HUGH R. ELWYN, Judge:

The petitioner, Franklin Pierce, the acknowledged father of an illegitimate child seeks to have defined and enforced his asserted right of visitation with his five year old daughter, [Joanna], which right the mother has, for the past year and a half, adamantly refused to recognize.

Custody of the child is not at issue. What is at issue is whether through de-emphasis of parental rights . . . and strict adherence to the "best interests of the child" criterion as conceived and defined by the mother alone, the court should permit the mother as custodial parent the prerogative of making the determination as to when and under what circumstances, if at all, the child may see her father, as is urged upon the court by her expert witness, or whether, the court should exercise its authority as *parens patriae* to temper the "best interests of the child" maxim with a recognition that the father of a child, even though illegitimate, has a right to association with his child which . . . must be recognized by the courts.

*   *   *

From the history of the relationship of these parents it is obvious that the child was not born of a casual relationship, but of one which endured for over two and a half years, and one in which, even after separation and up until shortly before her marriage [in July 1973], contact between father and daughter was actively encouraged by the mother. It is equally apparent that up until the time of the mother's marriage when the child's attitude toward her father completely changed that father and child enjoyed a mutually rewarding warm, loving father and daughter relationship.

Twice during the course of this lengthy proceeding which was begun in October 1973, the Court on application of the petitioner permitted him to take his daughter for visits to his home in Florida, the first time for two weeks in April 1974 and the second time for a month in July and August, upon condition that he post a cash bond in the amount of $10,000 to insure the return of the child to the mother's home and the jurisdiction of the Court. In each instance the petitioner readily complied with the condition and the child was returned to the mother's home at the appointed time.

At no time has there been any suggestion that the father is not a fit and capable custodian of his daughter or that when she has been temporarily in his custody is anything but well cared for. Indeed, the photographic evidence in this case shows that when the child has been in the father's custody she has been pampered with every luxury and attention a doting father can bestow.

The Court is completely satisfied that the petitioner is in all respect a wholly suitable and proper person to have the temporary care and custody of his daughter, even for an extended period of time. He has, through the creation of substantial trusts for the benefit of daughter, demonstrated his concern for her financial security and he has on two separate occasions demonstrated to the Court his financial responsibility. More importantly, he has also demonstrated his complete trustworthiness.

Thus, a decision in this case does not turn upon the fitness of either parent to be permanent or temporary custodian of the child, but rather upon whether in "the best interests of the child" she should be permitted some periodic association with her father or whether, as the mother would have it, she should be shielded from all further contact. To assist in resolving this issue both parties presented the testimony of psychiatrists.

Dr. Bernard F. Kalina, a psychiatrist, of Liberty, New York was called as a witness on behalf of the petitioner. Dr. Kalina who had examined the child at his office on March 12, 1974, pursuant to Court order, testified that he found the child to be very intelligent and bright with no mental disorders whatever. He expressed the opinion that the child loves her father; he thought that the child's negative feeling toward the father had developed because of the negative things the mother had said about the father and explained the child's change in attitude toward father by saying: "I feel her reactions would have to be negative since she loves Mommy and wants to please Mommy. If Mommy has said something negative about Franklin, certainly, in the presence of Mommy, she would have to act negatively."

Dr. Kalina further expressed the opinion that substantial visitation rights for the father "would be beneficial to the child. It would be especially beneficial if Mommy could be supportive of the visit. In terms of her growth and maturity, and she does, in my opinion, love Franklin and sharing these feelings towards one another would only lead to her growth about her feelings." The psychiatrist could see no reason why substantial visitation would be harmful to the child; on the contrary, he felt that a denial of further visits would in fact have a negative effect upon the child because the child would then feel rejected and confused and was firmly of the opinion that the child would benefit from such visits because such visits would be "important for her whole growth, mental, physical and spiritual."

* * *

Professor Solnit [on behalf of the respondent] conducted a clinical examination of Joanna on two occasions at the Yale University Child Study Center.

[T]he Professor said he found the child apprehensive and anxious and that it was his impression that she is under extraordinary tension. "She is anxious and she is insecure because of the experience she's had in which the visits of Mr.

Pierce are felt as a threat to her and are not
comfortable for her especially because she had to
leave home to visit Mr. Pierce soon after a new
baby had arrived in her family. I think that made
her very uncomfortable and uncertain and insecure."

Based upon these clinical observations, the
Professor then stated that "in (his) opinion,
Joanna's best interest would be served if she
could feel that Mr. and Mrs. Yerkovich were her
parents . . . [having] all the rights and privi-
leges of parents. . . . In other words, I believe
that she should not have the feeling that they lack
the authority or the ability to give her this security, of feeling wanted and permanent in her
family. . . ."

* * *

This is indeed, a novel and startling doctrine, and if accepted literally as Professor Solnit
and his co-authors Goldstein and Freud seriously
urge, would leave the court shorn of much of its
traditional role as *parens patriae* and guardian of
the child's best interest. Quite frankly, I do not
believe that the law of this State would tolerate
this Court, charged as it is with a responsibility
for the welfare of children, so supinely and ab-
jectly abdicating its function to any parent, however well intentioned. The danger and folly of
such a course is aptly illustrated by the circum-

stances of this case wherein a mother, who once permitted and actively encouraged free association between father and child, has, upon the contraction of a marriage, arbitrarily reversed her field and is now unwilling to permit any contact whatever between her daughter and the man who is the father of her child. The mother's change in attitude has, of course, been reflected in the child's attitude toward her father. The child, who was once outgoing, warm and loving, has become withdrawn, apprehensive and anxious and has on occasion referred to her father as a dirty rat. Such a change in a five year old child's attitude toward her father could only have been brought about through her mother's influence. Although she would no doubt deny it, the court can only conclude that the mother, consciously or unconsciously, now sees any enforced further association with her former paramour as an unwelcome reminder of her past indiscretion and as a threat to the stability and security of her marriage.

Consequently, the Court totally rejects the specious notion so ingenuously urged by Professor Solnit and his co-authors that the custodial parent should have the sole right to determine in the name of the best interests of the child whether the noncustodial parent should be permitted or denied association with his own child. Experience and common sense teach that, given the imperfections of human nature from which flow the bitterness and resentment which all too often accompany a marital or illicit love affair breakup, no one parent can, under such circumstances, be safely entrusted with a power so susceptible of abuse. . . .

Thus, we approach the central vital issue in this case. Is it in this child's best interest to be shielded by the mother from all future contact with her father, except through the mother's sufferance or do her best interests require that she should through her formative and growing up years have some continuing association with a father who has amply demonstrated his love and concern for his daughter? . . .

Any analysis of this situation brings one back to a fundamental truth which the psychiatrists, with all their talk of the psychological parent, have a tendency to overlook. Joanna, as is everyone, was born of two parents and, in my judgment, neither one has any God given exclusive right to control her destiny.

The concept of psychological parenthood should never be permitted to obscure the truth that "the natural father, as well as the natural mother, remains a parent no matter how estranged parent and child may become. . .

In spite of the circumstances of her birth, Joanna will one day have to come to grips with the fact that she does indeed have a father. As Dr. Kalina said, "Joanna will have to understand that father really exists as she grows older and learns to decide for herself". In the interim, he said, "it would be harmful if she wasn't allowed to see both parents".

The Special Guardian in her report to the court makes essentially the same point when she says that the mother's refusal of all visitation rights to the father "raises the question, not touched upon by the litigants, herein, of whether a child has a right to get to know and appreciate who her father is". She goes on to say: "Joanna's mother has admitted that Joanna does not know the circumstances of her birth, but the time will come when she must know. The real question is whether it will be too emotionally upsetting to Joanna to have the petitioner seeing her on a regular basis."

From her considerable personal contact with the child and both parents, the Special Guardian reports that she has "come to the conclusion that the respondent finds any contact whatsoever with the petitioner both distasteful and very upsetting and there is no question that this is communicated to her, whether consciously or not, to Joanna who is in turn upset and uneasy over the situation."

The Special Guardian concludes: "I am unable to accept Dr. Solnit's position which accords a father no rights whatsoever concerning his child if the mother determines that he should have none. I feel that if this is the case, somewhere along the line in her growth and development Joanna will be asking herself and those around her 'who am I' and 'where did I come from' and 'what is my father *really* like?' I feel that Joanna has a right to know and appreciate who her father is and what kind of a person he is, good or bad. On the other hand, I feel that it would serve no useful purpose to allow the petitioner such frequent visitation as to disrupt the peace, security and stability of the Yerkovich household.

"Joanna is a child of tender years and I agree with Dr. Solnit when he says that she has a need for stability and security. Also the fact that she is attending school now effectively prevents any visitation which will interfere with same."

It is the recommendation of the Special Guardian that the petitioner be granted limited visitation with the child away from the Yerkovich household but in the local area. . . .

The Court finds itself in accord with the views and recommendations of the Special Guardian. I do not share the fear of Professor Solnit that further contact of the child with her father will interfere with her development and her ability to think and relate to people. On the contrary, I fear that deprivation of future association with her natural father is more likely to stunt and warp her maturation and development as an emotionally stable adult. Her ability to think and relate to people is not going to be enhanced by shielding her from contact with them.

I hold these views because I am persuaded that in this particular case this father through his precept, counsel and example has much of value that he can contribute to the molding and shaping of his daughter's character and personality and that to deprive her of all association with her father, who has amply demonstrated his love and concern for her, would not be in her best interests.

The Court is aware that when visitation is renewed by the father such visits may cause the child some temporary emotional upset and perhaps some disruption of the Yerkovich household, but this is a price that must be paid if the child's larger long term interests are to be best served. Any emotional upset to this child occasioned by the presence of her father could be minimized if the mother would recognize the reality of the child's origins and be supportive of the tie that binds father and child together.

The willingness of the Court to afford this father an opportunity to permit Joanna to come once again to know, love and respect him as her father should not be regarded as novel. In fact, it but reflects the ancient wisdom of God's law as given to Moses on Mount Sinai wherein as the Fifth Commandment of the Decalogue it is written: "Honour thy father and thy mother: that thy days may be long upon the land which the Lord thy God giveth thee."

Consequently, in the exercise of discretion, the father is hereby accorded the right and privilege of visiting with his daughter Joanna on alternate weekends, a weekend being defined as from Friday evening at 5 P.M. to the following Sunday evening at 7 P.M., such visitation to take place away from the Yerkovich household and within the State of New York. In addition, the petitioner may have the temporary care and custody of his daughter for one month during the period from June 30 to September 1st of each year, with travel unrestricted.

Inasmuch as the petitioner has not been accorded the privilege of seeing his daughter since the summer of 1974, he is accorded the right and privilege of having his daughter with him on the weekend of December 20–22, and on alternate weekends thereafter.

Franklin Pierce took Joanna for a visit on that December 20, 1974. Her mother had no choice but to comply with the court's order. She described herself as

stripped of all power to protect my daughter. At 5:30 that afternoon, Franklin Pierce came to our door with a "witness" from the . . . law firm. Tears were streaming down Joanna's little face. She kept begging me to do something. I assured her that it was just for a couple of days and that before she knew it she would be home with us for Christmas. As I buttoned her coat, she repeated, "Please, Mommie, tell him to just leave me alone. I just want to stay with my family." Ray [Mrs. Yerkovich's husband, who wanted to adopt Joanna] stood outside our apartment door, and I persuaded Joanna to go with Franklin Pierce because she must obey the law. Outside the door she clung to her "Raymie's" leg for protection. Franklin Pierce seeing that Joanna would not go on her own physically pulled her away, flung her over his shoulder as she kicked and screamed in outrage. He carried my little daughter to his waiting Toyota station wagon, stuffed her into it and drove away.

Joanna was not returned on December 22, 1974, as the court order required. Since then and as of March, 1979, she has not been seen by her mother, sister, or stepfather.* These are cruel consequences of a system of justice that makes the child a pawn of the court, a victim of the simplistic notion that as *parens patriae* it has the capacity to manage and monitor better than a flesh-and-blood parent a child's growing up.[15]

---

* We do not suggest that children are usually not returned by noncustodial parents.

In this case, the court which had ordered the visits refused to use its offices to help Mrs. Yerkovich regain custody of Joanna; state law, as interpreted by state officials, apparently does not make such takings kidnapping and, therefore, their services were minimal. Beyond the state's boundaries, the F.B.I. claimed not to have jurisdiction since a putative father could not "kidnap" his own child.

Notes

CHAPTER 1: CHILD PLACEMENT IN PERSPECTIVE

1. See Phillipe Aries, *Centuries of Childhood* (New York: Alfred A. Knopf, 1962).

2. See Jeremy Bentham, *Theory of Legislation* (Boston: Weeks, Jordan, 1840, Vol. I, p. 248):

> The feebleness of infancy demands a continual protection. Everything must be done for an imperfect being, which as yet does nothing for itself. The complete development of its physical powers takes many years; that of its intellectual faculties is still slower. At a certain age, it has already strength and passions, without experience enough to regulate them. Too sensitive to present impulses, too negligent of the future, such a being must be kept under an authority more immediate than that of the laws. . . .

See also the opinion written in 1889 by Justice Brewer in *Chapsky* v. *Wood* (which we cite in Chapter 6).

CHAPTER 2: THE CHILD–PARENT RELATIONSHIPS

1. See Lillian Hellman, *An Unfinished Woman* (London: Penguin Books, 1972, pp. 12–13):

> There was a heavy fig tree on the lawn where the house turned the corner into the side street, and to the front and sides of the fig tree were three live oaks that hid the fig from my aunts' boarding-house. I suppose I was eight or nine before I discovered the pleasures of the fig tree. . . . The fig tree was heavy, solid, comfortable, and I had, through time, convinced myself that it wanted me, missed me when I was absent, and approved all the rigging I had done for the happy days I spent in its arms: I had made a sling to hold the school books, a pulley rope for my lunch basket, a hole for the bottle of afternoon cream-soda pop, a fishing pole and a smelly little bag of elderly bait, a pillow embroidered with a picture of Henry Clay on a horse that I had stolen from Mrs. Stillman, one of my aunts' boarders, and a proper nail to hold my dress and shoes to keep them neat for the return to the house.

2. E.g., a survey of the caseload of the Child Psychiatry Unit of the Yale University Child Study Center for the year 1972–1973 disclosed that 29 percent of the children were living only in one-parent families.

3. Determining a child's "biological" parents is not always easy. In cases of artificial insemination, for example, the donor of sperm may not be seen as a parent in any legal sense. See *Strnad* v. *Strnad,* 190 Misc. 786, 78 N.Y.S. 2d 390 (1948), cited in J. Goldstein and J. Katz, *The Family and the Law* (New York: Free Press, 1965, p. 501). Similarly, a woman might for money bear children for a childless couple, the husband's sperm being intro-

duced by artificial insemination. See "Girl Says She Had Baby for Mother," The *New York Times*, April 30, 1964 (p. 30, col. 1), cited in J. Goldstein and J. Katz (*supra*, p. 496).

   In the future, the development of artificial wombs and of reproduction by cloning may further blur the notion of biological parenthood.

The deficits in the psychological development of institutionalized infants (some of whom received excellent physical care) have been documented by many studies. See Margaret A. Ribble, *The Rights of Infants* (New York: Columbia University Press, 1943); W. Goldfarb, "Effects of Psychological Deprivation in Infancy and Subsequent Stimulation" (*American Journal of Psychiatry*, 102:18–33, 1945) and "Psychological Privation in Infancy and Subsequent Adjustment" (*American Journal of Orthopsychiatry*, 15:247–255, 1945); René A. Spitz, "Hospitalism" (*The Psychoanalytic Study of the Child*, 1:53–74; New York: International Universities Press, 1945) and "Hospitalism: A Follow-up Report" (*ibid.*, 2:113–117, 1946); René A. Spitz and K. M. Wolf, "Anaclitic Depression" (*ibid.*, 2:313–342, 1946); John Bowlby, *Maternal Care and Mental Health* (Geneva: World Health Organization Monograph No. 2, 1951); H. L. Rheingold, *The Modification of Social Responsiveness in Institutionalized Babies* (Monographs of the Society for Research in Child Development, Vol. XXI, Serial No. 63, No. 2, 1956); M. A. Ainsworth et al., *Deprivation of Maternal Care: A Reassessment of Its Effects* (Geneva: World Health Organization, Public Health Papers 14, 1962); Sally Provence and Rose C.

Lipton, *Infants in Institutions* (New York: International Universities Press, 1962).

5. See, e.g., Revised Uniform Adoption Act (1969), §14, Effect of Petition and Decree of Adoption:

   (a) A final decree of adoption and an interlocutory decree of adoption which has become final . . . have the following effect:

      (1) except with respect to a spouse of the petitioner and relatives of the spouse, to relieve the natural parents of the adopted individual of all parental rights and responsibilities, and to terminate all legal relationships between the adopted individual and his relatives, including his natural parents, so that the adopted individual therafter is a stranger to his former relatives for all purposes including inheritance and the interpretation or construction of documents, statutes, and instruments, whether executed before or after the adoption is decreed, which do not expressly include the individual by name or by some designation not based on a parent and child or blood relationship . . .

   If the adopted child is adopted again, the legal rights of the first set of adoptive parents are terminated, under the "relatives" language in §14 (a) (1) *supra*.

6. See, e.g., Revised Uniform Adoption Act (1969), §5, Persons Required to Consent to Adoption:

   (a) . . . a petition to adopt a minor may be granted

only if by written consent to a particular adoption has been executed by:

(1) the mother of the minor;

(2) the father of the minor, if the minor was conceived or born while the father was married to the mother, if the minor is his child by adoption, or if the minor has been established to be his child by his acknowledgment or a court proceeding. . . .

7. See, e.g., Revised Uniform Adoption Act (1969), §12, Required Residence of Minor:

> A final decree of adoption shall not be issued and an interlocutory decree of adoption does not become final, until the minor to be adopted, other than a stepchild of the petitioner, has lived in the adoptive home for at least 6 months after placement by an agency, or for at least 6 months after the [Public Welfare Department] or the Court has been informed of the custody of the minor by the petitioner, and the department or Court has had an opportunity to observe or investigate the adoptive home.

8. A similar attitude is often reflected in statutes. See, e.g., Subdivision 3 of Section 373 of the New York Social Welfare Law:

> "in granting orders of adoption . . . the court shall, when practicable, . . . give custody . . . only to . . . persons of the same religious faith as that of the child". See In re Maxwell's Adoption, 4 N.Y. 2d 429, 151 NE2d 848 (1958).

There is no comparable provision in the Revised Uniform Adoption Act (1969).

9.   See, e.g., *New Haven Register,* Thursday, November 2, 1972, p. 70, col. 1:

> Dear Ann Landers:
>
> The people who adopted me are the only parents I have ever known. They have been wonderful and everyone tells me how lucky I am.
>
> But there's this big break in my life. I need to find my real parents. I have to know what the circumstances were that made them give me away. My imagination runs wild when I think about what might have happened that made them abandon me.
>
> I think about these things more and more. It's getting so that I don't think about anything else. I have to learn the truth about myself so I can stop brooding. Don't tell me to forget it because I can't. I need some advice.
>
> —Confused in Chicago
>
> Dear Confused:
>
> It is natural for an adopted child to wonder about his blood parents—but you sound obsessed. If you were adopted through a legitimate agency it was agreed at the time that the identity of your natural parents would never be revealed—and with good reason. Usually when an adopted child locates his natural parents it means trouble—both for the child and for the adoptive parents. I won't tell you to "forget it" but I do hope for the sake of everyone concerned that you will not make this your life's goal. Do

yourself a favor and divert your thoughts to something more productive and less hazardous.

See also *New Haven Register*, Tuesday, February 20, 1973, p. 38, Col. 3–4:

Dear Ann:
May I speak to the young man who wants to find his real parents?

Dear Confused: If you were the baby I gave away, don't come knocking on my door. You have no real parents here. Your REAL parents are the loving couple who wanted a child. I didn't.

Frankly, I think you are selfish to want two families. Count your blessings and don't look back. The parents who raised you love you and they are entitled to your total devotion. Forget about me.   —Straight Arrow

10.   See, e.g., "Foster Parents' Manual," of the Jewish Child Care Association of New York, reprinted in J. Goldstein and J. Katz, *The Family and the Law* (*supra*, pp. 1019ff.).

11.   See, e.g., "Placement Agreement" of the Jewish Child Care Association of New York:

5. We acknowledge that we are accepting the child placed with us for an indeterminate period, depending on the needs of the child or his family situation. We are aware that the legal responsibility for the foster child remains with the Agency, and we will accept and comply with any plans the Agency makes for the child. This

> includes the right to determine when and how
> the child leaves us, and we agree to cooperate
> with arrangements made toward that end.

Reprinted from J. Goldstein and J. Katz (*supra*, p. 1022).
See also Connecticut's "Agreement for Board and Care
of Children Committed to the State Welfare Commissioner," which provides:

> In consideration of receiving a child
> [born on . . .] into my family home from the
> State Welfare Commission I . . . residing at . . .
> do hereby agree with the State Welfare Commis-
> sioner that so long as said child shall be within
> my care:

> 1. Said child shall be given sufficient and
>   suitable food, bed, and shall not be re-
>   quired to perform an amount of labor
>   unsuitable for his age and strength.
> 2. Said child shall be given full opportunity
>   to attend school during the terms and
>   hours prescribed by the laws of the state
>   and the rules of the State Board of Edu-
>   cation.
> 3. Said child shall be given full opportunity
>   to attend religious services and receive
>   instruction in the [designated] faith.
> 4. Said child shall receive necessary medi-
>   cal care as provided on the other side of
>   the Agreement. All accidents and ill-
>   nesses of said child will be immediately
>   reported by me to the State Welfare Com-
>   missioner at the nearest district office.

6. It is clearly understood that this child is placed on a board and care basis only and is not placed with me for adoption.

7. The name of said child shall not be changed except by the approval of the State Welfare Commissioner and by application to the superior court, as provided by Section 52-11 of the General Statutes, Revision of 1958, and notice shall be given to said State Welfare Commissioner whenever a change of name is made.

8. The State Welfare Commissioner reserves the right to remove said child at any time from the above mentioned home and upon such removal this agreement is cancelled immediately.

[Financial] terms: . . .

12. See, e.g., testimony in *In re Jewish Child Care Association*, Supreme Court, New York, before Justice Cortland A. Johnson, Nov. 22, 1957:

> [Doctor Miller, an officer of the Child Care Association] testified that the objection of the agency at this point is that Mr. and Mrs. Sanders [foster parents] have become too emotionally involved with the child and that it would be better for the child, who ultimately, she says, will be with the natural mother—this is something that will happen in the future; we do not know when—that it would be better for her to be placed in a neutral home, a home where she

> would be liked, but not loved, to the degree that
> the Sanderses love her. . . .

Reprinted from J. Goldstein and J. Katz (*supra,* p. 1029).

13.   Note the encouraging direction of the recent New York
      Court decision cited in Chapter 3, note 14 (*infra*). See
      also our discussion concerning the *Rothman* case in
      Chapter 6 (*infra*).

14.   See, e.g., Thesi Bergmann in collaboration with Anna
      Freud, *Children in the Hospital* (New York: Interna-
      tional Universities Press, 1965, pp. 22–23):

> Psychoanalytic child psychology leaves
> no doubt that children are emotionally depen-
> dent on their parents and that this dependence
> is necessary for purposes of normal develop-
> ment; also, that relationships in a hospital are,
> at best, poor substitutes for family relationships.
> Once these facts are accepted, relaxation of visit-
> ing rules becomes an inevitable consequence.
>
> In Rainbow [Hospital], parents were
> given every opportunity to visit their children
> any time they liked, and to observe them during
> stressful as well as during easy times, in periods
> of physical therapy, pool activity, exercises,
> school, play, etc. Care was taken that parents
> and children could interact as they do at home,
> a child occasionally preferring to play with other
> children while the mother visited with other
> mothers or the nurse. Young children were espe-
> cially eager to be put to bed and tucked in by
> their mothers, while older children preferred to

be up with their visitors as long as possible. When there were no epidemics in the community, siblings visited on Sunday, which often became "picnic day" for the whole family in the hospital grounds.

Family ties were maintained further by the children making telephone calls to their homes and by all, except those in body casts, if they had progressed sufficiently in convalescence, going home occasionally for weekends. The latter visits were effective in teaching the child to cope with his disabilities under the less protective circumstances of a normal home, to mix with friends and neighbors after a prolonged absence, to be seen by them in a wheel chair, walking with braces or crutches, etc. Parents became accustomed in this manner to deal on their own with the responsibility of caring for a frail or handicapped child and to master their own anxieties.

15. In some cases in some states, a foster child who is not legally adopted may still participate in the estate of an intestate foster parent, taking under a label such as "equitable" or "virtual" adoption, or "adoption" by estoppel. See Jeffries, "Equitable Adoption: They Took Him Into Their Home and Called Him Fred," 58 *Va. L. R.* 727 (1972). But see *Proffitt* v. *Evans*, 433 S.W. 2nd 876 (Ky. 1968): "The common law did not provide for adoptions. Strict compliance with the adoption statutes has always been required. . . . To recognize a 'de facto' adoption would bring a condition of chaos to the law."

16. *Painter* v. *Bannister* 140 N.W. 2d 152 (Iowa 1966) is an interesting celebrated case in point. There, in a *habeas corpus* action, a biological father sought to regain the custody of his seven-year-old son, whom he had left with the child's maternal grandparents (following his wife's death in an automobile accident two and one half years earlier). The household of the grandparents was described as "stable, dependable, conventional, middle-class, midwest" and that of the biological parent as "unstable, unconventional, arty Bohemian, and probably intellectually stimulating." "It is not our prerogative," the appellate court asserted, "to determine custody upon our choice of one of two ways of life within normal and proper limits and we will not do so." It concurred with the trial judge's finding that both parties were proper and fit to serve as parents. While acknowledging a preference in law for the biological parent, the court weighed more heavily the child's welfare and concluded that the existing psychological parent-child relationship should not be disturbed.

> Mark has established a father-son relationship with [the grandfather] which he apparently had never had with his natural father. He is happy, well-adjusted and progressing nicely in his development. We do not believe it is for Mark's best interest to take him out of this stable atmosphere in the face of warnings of dire consequences from an eminent child psychologist and send him to an uncertain future in his father's home. Regardless of our appreciation of the father's love for his child and his desire to have him with him, we do not believe we have

the moral right to gamble with this child's future ... [*id.* at 158].

17. These guidelines also have substantial implications for child placement in juvenile deliquency proceedings; however, those implications are not explored in this volume.

18. For more detailed descriptions see, e.g., Anna Freud, *The Ego and the Mechanisms of Defense* (New York: International Universities Press [1936], rev. ed., 1966) and *Normality and Pathology in Childhood* (*ibid.*, 1965); D. W. Winnicott, *Mother and Child* (New York: Basic Books, 1957); Milton E. Senn and Albert J. Solnit, *Problems in Child Behavior* (Philadelphia: Lea & Febiger, 1968); and Sally Provence, *Guide for the Care of Infants in Groups* (New York: Child Welfare League of America, 1967).

CHAPTER 3:   ON CONTINUITY, A CHILD'S SENSE OF TIME, AND THE LIMITS OF BOTH LAW AND PREDICTION

1. A large number of the children billeted without their families in wartime England developed enuresis. Many specific examples of regression following separation are recorded by Anna Freud and Dorothy Burlingham in *Infants Without Families: Reports on the Hampstead Nurseries* (*The Writings of Anna Freud*, Volume III. New York: International Universities Press, 1973).

2. A not uncommon case history of this sort is found in *Carter* v. *United States*, 252 F. 2d 608 (D.C. Cir. 1957), reprinted in R. C. Donnelly, J. Goldstein, and R. D.

Schwartz, *Criminal Law* (New York: Free Press, 1962, pp. 784–788):

> Carter was indicted, tried, convicted, and sentenced to death for first-degree murder. . . .
>
> At the time of the offense Carter was eighteen years of age. . . .
>
> . . . Carter spent the first seven or eight years of his life with his father's sister, a blind woman. . . .
>
> . . . Carter's aunt released him to the Child Welfare Division of the Department of Public Welfare. He was forced to leave his first foster home. After six months at a second foster home he was placed with a Mr. and Mrs. Reed, with whom he stayed about four years. The Reeds found him extremely difficult. He relieved himself in his clothing and bedclothing "just as regularly as if it were the right thing." He often struck smaller children without provocation. . . .
>
> Carter left the Reeds in August, 1949, and went to the Industrial Home School at Blue Plains. While there, he forced a child into an act of sodomy, threw a knife at another child, and was in the habit of fighting with smaller children who would not give him their possessions. . . . Upon reaching the age of sixteen (in December, 1952) Carter was placed in another foster home. He stayed there only a short time and then went to live with a Mrs. Gordon, who requested the authorities to remove him from her home after he masturbated in her presence.
>
> Thereafter Carter moved to still another

foster home for about one month, after which
he was again placed in yet another foster home
where he remained for three days and then ran
away. He was found seventeen days later . . .
and was removed to a Receiving Home for Children. He subsequently left the Receiving Home
to live with his father, remaining there about
one month. . . . He was apprehended on a com-
plaint charging "disorderly conduct or peeping
tom" and was sent back to the Receiving
Home. . . .

3. See Carl Pollock and Brandt F. Steele, "A Therapeutic
    Approach to the Parents." In: *Helping the Battered
    Child and His Family,* ed. by C. Henry Kempe and Ray
    E. Helfer (Philadelphia: J. B. Lippincott, 1972, pp. 3–
    22); and Brandt F. Steele, "Parental Abuse of Infants
    and Small Children." In: *Parenthood: Its Psychology
    and Psychopathology,* ed. by E. James Anthony and
    Therese Benedek (Boston: Little Brown & Co., 1970, pp.
    449–479); and S. Wasserman, "The Abused Parent of
    the Abused Child" (*Children,* 14:5, 1967).

4. Adoption, even when "final," may be conditional and
    thus in effect subject to the continuing jurisdiction of the
    courts with power to abrogate. See, e.g., *New York Do-
    mestic Relations Law,* §118-a (1970) which provides in
    pertinent part:

    > [Any adoptive child] . . . or any person or
    > authorized agency on behalf of such child may
    > make an application to a judge or surrogate of
    > the court in which the original adoption took
    > place for the abrogation of such adoption on the

ground of (a) cruelty, (b) misusage, (c) inability or refusal to support, maintain, or educate such child, (d) *an attempt to change or the actual making of change of or the failure to safeguard the religion of such child* or (e) any other violation of duty on the part of the adoptive parents or parent toward such child [our italics].

5. The Uniform Adoption Act of 1953 provided in Optional §17 that adoptive parents could petition to annul "If within two years after the adoption a child develops any serious and permanent physical or mental malady or incapacity as a result of conditions existing prior to the adoption and of which the adopting parents had no knowledge or notice. . . ."

    The Revised Uniform Adoption Act (1969) has no such provision.

    But see Kentucky Rev. Stat. §199.540(1) (1969) which provides that an adoption can be set aside by a decree of annulment if within five years the adopted child "reveals definite traits of ethnological ancestry different from those of the adoptive parents, and of which the adoptive parents had no knowledge or information prior to the adoption. . . ."

6. We thus reject the approach taken in the Revised Uniform Adoption Act (1969) which requires a period of at least six months after an agency placement before an adoption decree can become final—a longer period is required for other adoptions (Section 12) and an appeal procedure based on that used in ordinary civil actions (Section 15(a)).

    For the provisions of Section 12, see Chapter 2, note 7 (*supra*). Section 15 provides:

15. [Appeal and Validation of Adoption Decree.]
   (a) An appeal from any final order or decree rendered under this Act may be taken in the manner and time provided for appeal from a [judgment in a civil action].
   (b) Subject to the disposition of an appeal, upon the expiration of [one] year after an adoption decree is issued the decree cannot be questioned by any person including the petitioner, in any manner upon any ground, including fraud, misrepresentation, failure to give any required notice, or lack of jurisdiction of the parties or of the subject matter, unless, in the case of the adoption of a minor, or, in the case of the adoption of an adult, the adult had no knowledge of the decree within the [one] year period.

7. §409(a) of the Uniform Marriage and Divorce Act compromises the continuity concept while trying to respond to it by providing fixed intervals during which decrees may not be modified:

> No motion to modify a custody decree may be made earlier than one year after the date of the initial decree. If a motion for modification has been filed, whether or not it was granted, no subsequent motion may be filed within 2 years after disposition of the prior motion, unless the court decides . . . that there is reason to believe that the child's present environment may en-

danger his physical health or significantly impair his emotional development.

This problem may · be greatly exacerbated by conflicting laws between states and between countries. See, e.g., Uniform Adoption Act, §14.

8. If the interrupting visits are not allowed by the custodian, the court may, on that ground alone, create further discontinuity by changing the child's custodian. See, e.g., *Berlin* v. *Berlin* 239 Md. 52, 210A. 2d 380 (1965), where the child is awarded to the father for the sole reason that the mother had not lived up to the visitation requirements of the initial decree which granted her custody. But see *Berlin* v. *Berlin* 21 N.Y. 2d 371, 235 N.E. 2d 109 (1967), in which the New York court refused to honor the Maryland court order to change custody.

9. We would thus oppose such provisions as the following from the Uniform Marriage and Divorce Act:

§407. [Visitation.]
   (a) A parent not granted custody of the child is entitled to reasonable visitation rights unless the court finds, after a hearing, that visitation would endanger the child's physical health or significantly impair his emotional development.
   (b) The court may modify an order granting or denying visitation rights whenever modification would serve the best interests of the child; but the court shall not restrict a parent's visitation rights unless

> danger the child's physical health or sig-
> nificantly impair his emotional develop-
> ment.

§408. [Judicial Supervision.]
> (a) Except as otherwise agreed by the parties
> in writing at the time of the custody de-
> cree, the custodian may determine the
> child's upbringing, including his educa-
> tion, health care, and religious training,
> unless the court after hearing, finds,
> upon motion by the non-custodial par-
> ent, that in the absence of a specific
> limitation of the custodian's authority,
> the child's physical health would be en-
> dangered or his emotional development
> significantly impaired.

10. It is of interest that much of what we have said in the
preceding paragraphs is also contained in The Civil Code
of Japan (Supreme Court of Japan, Tokyo, Official English Translation, pp. 152–153), which, e.g., provides:

> Article 818. A child who had not yet
> attained majority is subject to the parental
> power of its father and mother. . . .

> While the father and mother are in
> matrimonial relation, they jointly exercise the
> parental power. But, if either the father or the
> mother is unable to exercise the parental power,
> the other parent exercises it.

> Article 819. If father and mother have
> effected divorce by agreement, they shall deter-
> mine one of them to have the parental power by
> agreement.

In case of judicial divorces the Court determines a father or mother to have the parental power.

If the father and mother have effected divorce before the birth of child, the parental power is exercised by the mother. But the father and mother may determine the father to have the parental power by agreement after the birth of child. . . .

If no agreement mentioned in any of pars. 1 and 3 and preceding paragraph is reached or possible, the Family Court may render judgment in place of agreement on application of the father or mother. . . .

Section II.   Effect of Parental Power

Article 820.   A person who exercises parental power has the rights and incurs the duty of providing for the custody and education of his or her child.

Article 821.   A child must establish its place of residence in the place designated by the person who exercises parental power.

11. The lack of finality and the "continuity" of discontinuity pending appeal is dramatically illustrated by the following case reported in the *London Times* (February 16, 1973, p. 6, col. 6):

NEW DIVORCE PROCEEDINGS PROLONG
DESRAMAULT CASE

The case for the custody of Caroline Desramault, who has been a bone of contention for three years between her divorced English mother and French father, has taken yet another legal turn.

It seemed to have been settled finally by the Cour de Cassation's rejection on Tuesday, of M Desramault's appeal against the court decision giving custody of Caroline to her mother. However, the whole ponderous legal machine has been set in motion again by way of new divorce proceedings before the Versailles court.

The Versailles court in May, 1971, had ruled in a provisional order that Caroline should be entrusted for three-monthly periods to her father and mother alternately. M Desramault did not accept this judgment and refused to hand over the child. Two months later the Court of Appeal in Paris annulled the provisional order by the Versailles court and, pending a final decision, entrusted the custody of Caroline to Mme Desramault, her paternal grandmother.

M Desramault wanted to keep the child and hid her. The grandmother then started a new action, and a new judgment entrusted custody of the child provisionally to the father.

In July last year the Versailles tribunal, which had to give a new judgment on the divorce proceedings because the first one was annulled by the Paris Court of Appeals, ordered a new investigation and temporarily entrusted the custody of the child to the mother.

The father, however, fled with the child to Switzerland, and on an action by the mother a Swiss court placed the child in a home, the address of which is kept secret.

12. But see decision of Judge Polier in *In re Sylvia Clear* 58 Misc. 2d 699, 296 N.Y.S. 2d 184 (Fam. Ct. Juv. Term N.Y. Co. 1969) in which she describes the dangers inherent in the N.Y. Family Ct. Act §611 which requires child care agencies to make "diligent efforts to encourage and strengthen the parental relationships." In that case the court describes the negative reaction of a child in foster placement to her biological parent's visits which were sponsored in accord with the statute by the child care agency. The right of visitation can, at least as time goes by, become a problem in what initially is perceived as temporary foster placement.

13. In "Young Children in Brief Separation: A Fresh Look" (*The Psychoanalytic Study of the Child*, 26:264–315, New York: Quadrangle Books, 1971) James and Joyce Robertson compare two forms of substitute care for young children whose mothers were confined to the hospital. One group of children received foster care in the home of the Robertsons; another child was placed in a residential nursery. See also the films made by James and Joyce Robertson, *Young Children in Brief Separation* (films Nos. 1, 2, and 4; London: Tavistock Child Development Research Unit; New York: New York University Film Library, 1967–1971) and *John: 17 Months* (film No. 3, *ibid.*, 1969).

14. See, e.g., the dissent of Judge Froessel in *In re Jewish Child Care Association*, 5 N.Y. 2d 222, 156 N.Y. 2d 700 (1959):

> Laura was born on June 3, 1953. Her mother delivered her to the Department of Wel-

fare of New York City, who thereupon turned
her over to the Agency. On July 30, 1954 the
Agency gave the child to the Sanders for board-
ing care, at which time she was not quite 14
months old. . . . Laura's mother visited her but
once a year for the first two years. Small wonder
then that the Sanders thought she had little interest in Laura, and therefore inquired about
adopting her, despite the fact that they had been
told by the Agency that Laura could not be
adopted. Its order having been disobeyed, the
Agency sought to place the child in another
home. The Sanders were told they "were too attached to the child"; they "loved her too much."
For that entirely normal human reaction of the
average person to the love of a child, Laura is
to be transferred to strangers in the sixth year
of her life. . . . If Laura is to be bandied about
meanwhile from family to family until she is
transferred to her mother, each such change will
be extremely difficult for the child, as testified
to without contradiction by the psychiatrist at
the hearing. Why multiply the shocks? And if
the mother never chooses to take Laura, and
that does not appear to be unlikely from the
record before us, the child could not find a better home than she now enjoys.

15. See, e.g., the Connecticut agreement, which clearly spe-
cifies the financial terms (Chapter 2, note 11, *supra*).

16. For an explanation of such a program established in
Maryland, see "Guidelines for Subsidized Adoption"

issued on July 15, 1969 by the State Department of Social Services:

1. Subsidized Adoption—General Intent

Subsidizing adoption is a method which makes it possible for potential parents to adopt a child for whom they can supply all the requisites of good parental care except the financial ability to support an additional dependent. Subsidization opens up additional resources for many children for whom there are insufficient adoption homes. A home with subsidy payment will be considered for any child for whom this is the best placement resource.

The adoptive family may either be the foster parents of the child or they may be adoptive applicants.

Subsidization, which makes possible permanency and continuity of care and affection, provides important benefits to the child. The agency will usually have guardianship of the child in preadoptive care, with the right to consent to adoption or to adoption and/or long-term care. Some children will have been in regular foster care with no family ties or contacts with parents over a prolonged period of time and for these children guardianship will be obtained, so that adoption may be consummated by the foster families in which the children are settled, or adoptive placement may be made with a new family, depending on the individual situation. It is to be expected that many of the chil-

dren will be those who were hard to place because they were part of a sibling group, or
because of age, minority race or handicap.

Reprinted in Monrad G. Paulsen, Walter Wadlington,
Julius Goebel, Jr., *Domestic Relations* (Mineola, N.Y.:
Foundation Press, 1970, pp. 737f.).

17. See, e.g., Anna Freud and Dorothy Burlingham, *Infants
Without Families: Reports on the Hampstead Nurseries*
(*The Writings of Anna Freud,* Vol. III. New York: International Universities Press, 1973, pp. 182–183) where
they describe the violent reactions of a small child to
the parting of his mother:

> The child feels suddenly deserted by all the
> known persons in his world to whom he has
> learned to attach importance. His new ability
> to love finds itself deprived of the accustomed
> objects, and his greed for affection remains un-
> satisfied. His longing for his mother becomes
> intolerable and throws him into states of despair
> which are very similar to the despair and dis-
> tress shown by babies who are hungry and whose
> food does not appear at the accustomed time.
> For several hours or even for a day or two this
> psychological craving of the child, the "hunger"
> for his mother, may override all bodily sensa-
> tions. There are some children of this age who
> will refuse to eat or to sleep. Very many of them
> will refuse to be handled or comforted by
> strangers.
>
> The children cling to some object or to
> some form of expression which means to them

at that moment memory of the material presence of the mother. Some will cling to a toy which the mother has put into their hands at the moment of parting; others to some item of bedding or clothing which they have brought from home. Some will monotonously repeat the word by which they are used to call their mothers. . . .

Observers seldom appreciate the depth and seriousness of this grief of a small child. Their judgment of it is misled for one main reason. This childish grief is short-lived. Mourning of equal intensity in an adult person would have to run its course throughout a year; the same process in the child between 1 and 2 years will normally be over in 36 to 48 hours. It is a psychological error to conclude from this short duration that the reaction is only a superficial one and can be treated lightly.

See also Anna Freud, "The Concept of the Rejecting Mother" (*The Writings of Anna Freud*, Vol. IV. New York: International Universities Press, 1968, pp. 596–597):

The first attempt at object love has been destroyed; the next one will not be of quite the same quality, will be more demanding, more intent on immediate wish fulfillments, i.e., further removed from the more mature forms of "love."

18.   See, e.g., *In re Lem* 164 A. 2d 345 (D.C. Mun. Ct. App. 1960):

[Rover, C. J.] The mother of Cecelia Lem, . . . appeals from an order committing her daughter to the legal custody and guardianship of the Department of Public Welfare until her 21st birthday, and permanently depriving her of custody in order that the Welfare Department may consent to the adoption of the child. . . .

The child was born January 11, 1956. Paternity has not been established. . . . For about four months after the birth of the child a private social welfare agency sought to advise the mother as to the best course for her to follow, but she resisted any definite planning other than foster care for the child. At the expiration of four months, and apprehending that long-term planning would be required, the agency referred the case to the Department of Public Welfare. On May 4, 1956, the child came into "emergency care" of the Child Welfare Division of the Welfare Department and was placed in a home for infants.

During the next 14 months the Division sought either to work out a plan whereby the mother would actively assume custody and responsibility for her child, or to persuade her to surrender it for adoption. She cooperated with the Division so long as she was not forced to make a definite decision. When pressed for some definitive action, however, she would state that her psychiatrist had cautioned her about being "rushed" into making a decision, and would become uncommunicative, withdrawn and unavailable.

On July 3, 1957, the Child Welfare Division, pursuant to the provisions of Code 1951, §11-908, filed a petition in the Juvenile Court charging that the child was without adequate parental care. Code 1951 §11-906(a)(6). In an accompanying report it related the mother's history of vacillation and indecisiveness concerning the rearing of the child and recommended that the latter be committed to the Department of Public Welfare for three months "in order to give the mother this additional time either to make her decision to release Cecelia for permanent planning or to offer a satisfactory plan of care for her independent of Child Welfare Division." On July 10, 1957, a hearing was held with the mother's court-appointed counsel present; the court found the child was without adequate parental care and committed her to the Department of Public Welfare until October 9, 1957. This period appears to have been inadquate to accomplish its purpose, and the court on November 11, 1957, after a hearing with the mother and counsel present, committed the child to the Welfare Department for two years until November 4, 1959. The mother consented to this action.

At the end of the latter commitment period a hearing was again held on November 25, 1959. At that time counsel for the mother indicated it was his intention to ask for more time for his client to formulate her plans. The court replied that it would hear no arguments for further temporary commitment, but would confine the hearing to resolving the issue of permanent custody in the mother or the Welfare Department. Counsel for the mother acquiesced in this ruling and the hearing proceeded on that basis.

. . . The mother visited her about once every two months throughout the period. . . .

The mother herself testified that she loved her daughter very much and had developed a close attachment for her during her visits; she also expressed concern about the child's welfare. She said she never thought about the possibility that the child would be taken from her, but since that was the course this hearing was taking, she was now willing to assume custody and responsibility for the child rather than lose her permanently.

This was the first time she evidenced any decisiveness in the matter, and thus we have pointed up the fundamental issue in this case—whether her decision has come too late. The child was by then almost four years old and so far as the record indicates, never had been under the care of the mother for any length of time. . . .

. . . At the conclusion of the hearing the court ruled against the mother. . . .

No reasonable mind could question the proposition that a child deprived of the care and attention of its natural mother and committed to the care of welfare agencies for the first four years of its life is a neglected child within the meaning of the statute. We think the evidence was completely adequate to sustain the court's finding.

19. See, e.g., *O'Brien* v. *Brown*, 409 U.S. 1 (1972) (presidential primary-political process); *New York Times* v. *United States*, 403 U.S. 713 (1971) (national security and freedom of speech); *Freedman* v. *Maryland*, 380 U.S. 51 (1964) (freedom of speech); *Cooper* v. *Aaron*, 358 U.S. 1 (1958) (right to education); *Youngstown Co.* v. *Sawyer*, 343 U.S. 579 (1951) (national security); *United States* v. *United Mine Workers*, 330 U.S. 258 (1947) (national security).

20. See, e.g., *In re Clark* 210.0.2d 86, 90 O.L.A. 21 (1962):

> [Kenneth Clark, aged 3 years, was suffering second and third degree burns over 40 percent of his body.] [T]he child's parents refused to authorize [blood transfusions] because the religious sect to which they belong (Jehovah's Witnesses) forbids it. . . . Ohio's Juvenile Code empowers the Juvenile Court to protect the rights of a child in this condition:
>
>> § 2152.33, Revised Code. * * * Upon the certificate of one or more reputable practicing physicians, the court may summarily provide for emergency medical and surgical treatment which appears to be immediately necessary for any child concerning whom a complaint or an application for care has been filed, pending the service of a citation upon its parents, guardian, or custodian. * * *
>
> Even without this specific authorization we believe the court would have had ample power to act summarily under its broad equitable jurisdiction.

And see *Georgetown College Inc.* 221 F.2d 1000, n. 15, p. 1007 (D.C. Cir. 1964) Cert. den. 377 U.S. 978 (1964)

21. *Freedman* v. *Maryland* 380 U.S. 51, 58–59 (1964). The court refers to a New York procedure which if applied to child placement, not film censorship, would preclude interruption of an ongoing relationship until a hearing before a court which must be provided one day after notice of the dispute about placement is given; the judge must hand down his decision within two days after termination of the hearing. *Id.* at 60. No mention is made of similarly expeditious determinations on appeal. Such provisions would, of course, have to be made in child placement.

22. Ner Littner, "Discussion of a Program of Adoptive Placement for Infants under Three Months" (*American Journal of Orthopsychiatry,* 26:577, 1956).

23. Such a proposal comports with the concept of divisible divorce which recognizes that the official severance of personal relationships between the adult parties is divisible from (and need not be conditioned on or await a final determination of) property and support rights. *Estin* v. *Estin,* 334 U.S. 541 (1948). Where an adult party to a divorce has sought to preclude a final decree of divorce until a final property settlement has been reached, courts have observed, e.g., "society will be little concerned if the parties engage in property litigation of however long duration; it will be much concerned if two people are forced to remain legally bound to one another when this status can do nothing but engender additional bitterness and unhappiness." *Hall* v. *Superior Court of*

Los Angeles County, 54 Cal. 2d 139 352 P2d 161 (1960). Ending disputes about the child-adult relationships seems equally if not a more compelling reason for invoking the divisible divorce concept. *May* v. *Anderson*, 345 U.S. 528 (1953). That concept is implicit in the continuing jurisdiction courts retain over custody decisions, which, of course, we oppose.

24. The model statutory provisions which we propose in Chapter 7 are more specific.

25. See 35 ALR 2d 662, 668 (1954) and *Winans* v. *Luppie* 47 N.J. Eq. 302, 305 (1890) ; Hazuke's case 345 Pa. 432 (1942) ; and *Lott* v. *Family and Children's Society*, Sup. Ct. of N.J. (1953) reprinted in J. Goldstein and J. Katz, *The Family and the Law* (*supra*, p. 1115).

26. See, e.g., the N.Y. Family Ct. Act. Art. VI, §611 which provides in pertinent part: "permanent neglect [is established when] the parent . . . has failed for a period for more than one year following the placement . . . substantially and continuously or repeatedly to maintain contact with and plan for the future of the child, although physically and financially able to do so, not withstanding the [child care] agency's diligent efforts to encourage and strengthen the parental relationship."

27. Judge Polier, construing the provision in *In re Sylvia Clear*, 58 Misc. 2d 699, 296 N.Y.S. 2d 184 (Fam. Ct. Juv. Term N.Y. Co. 1969) with regard to a case worker's decision not to encourage visits by a biological mother (see note 12 *supra*), said:

Visits with the mother were soon seen as disturbing to the child. . . . There is no basis for criticizing the action of the agency whose first responsibility was the well-being of the child. The agency could not have sought to strengthen the parental relationship without violating its responsibility for the welfare of the child in its custody. Yet that is what the present statute requires as a condition to terminating parental rights.

Although this court is satisfied it would be in the best interest of the child to terminate parental rights, it cannot find that the statute empowers it to do so. The mother has continued to visit this child, has persistently rejected the idea of surrender, and the mother continues to speak of making a home for both her children in the future when she feels stronger. While this courts finds no evidence to sustain this expressed hope and is satisfied that the mother is not competent to care for this child, the evidence does not warrant a finding that the present statutory requirement has been met.

28.   See, e.g., California Civil Code §232a (1961) which provides in pertinent part:

Sec. 232.   Persons entitled to be declared free from parental custody and control. An action may be brought for the purpose of having any person under the age of 21 years declared free from the custody and control of either or both of his parents when such person . . . has been left by either or both of his parents

in the care and custody of another without any
provision for his support, or without communica-
tion from either or both of his parents, for the
period of one year with the intent on the part
of such parent or parents to abandon such person. Such failure to provide, or such failure to
communicate for the period of one year, shall be
presumptive evidence of the intent to abandon.

29.   See, e.g., *Davies Adoption Case* 353 Pa. 579 (1946). *In re
Graham* 239 Mo. App. 1036 (1947).

30.   While the process through which a new child-parent
status emerges is too complex and subject to too many
individual variations for the law to know just when
"abandonment" may have occurred, the law can generally verify that the biological tie never matured into an
affirmative psychological tie for the child or that a developing psychological tie has been broken or damaged
and whether a promising new relationship has developed
and is being formed.

31.   See Jeremy Bentham, *Theory of Legislation* (*supra*,
1840, Vol. I, p. 254).

[T]he natural arrangement, which leaves the
choice, the mode, and the burden of education to
the parents, may be compared to a series of ex-
periments for perfecting the general system.
Every thing is advanced and developed by the
emulation of individuals, and by differences of
ideas and of genius; in a word, by the variety
of particular impulses. But let the whole be cast
into a single mould; let instruction everywhere

take the form of legal authority; errors will be perpetuated, and there will be no further progress. . . .

32. It has taken the law a long time, for example, to realize that its power to deny divorce cannot establish a healthy marriage, or preclude the parties from separating, or even prevent new "relationships" from maturing. See J. Goldstein and M. Gitter, "On the Abolition of Grounds for Divorce: A Model Statute and Commentary" (*Family Law Quart.*, 3:75–99, 1969).

33. See *Lott* v. *Family and Children's Society* (cited in note 25, *supra*).

34. The law, seeking to safeguard the privacy of family relationships and the private ordering of one's life, has adopted a policy of minimum state intervention consistent, of course, with the state's goal of safeguarding the well-being of children, protecting them from exploitation by adults. See J. Goldstein and M. Gitter (*supra*, note 32). See also Justice Douglas's dissent in *Wisconsin* v. *Yoder* (cited in Chapter 5, note 3, *infra*).

35 See, e.g., J. D. Watson, professor of molecular biology at Harvard (*New York Times*, March 22, 1973, col. 3, p. 43):

We must never forget that for the most part we have little insight about the truly unknown—the world we live in is immensely complicated and on the whole its natural phenomena are remarkably unpredictable. Only after a chemical reaction within a cell has been observed, do we

> usually find a reason for its existence. Thus it is almost impossible to plan far ahead what the future will bring.

36. See Anna Freud, "Child Observation and Prediction of Development: A Memorial Lecture in Honor of Ernst Kris" (*The Psychoanalytic Study of the Child*, Vol. 13, pp. 97–98; New York: International Universities Press, 1958):

> I name three [factors which] make prediction difficult and hazardous. (1) There is no guarantee that the rate of maturational progress on the side of ego development and drive development will be an even one; and whenever one side of the structure outdistances the other in growth, a variety of unexpected and unpredictable deviations from the norm will follow. (2) There is still no way to approach the quantitative factor in drive development, nor to foresee it; but most of the conflict solutions within the personality will, in the last resort, be determined by quantitative rather than by qualitative factors. (3) The environmental happenings in a child's life will always remain unpredictable since they are not governed by any known laws.

CHAPTER 4:   ON THE LEAST DETRIMENTAL ALTERNATIVE

1. For a codification of the ambiguity and ambivalence which have come to surround this standard see §402 of the Uniform Marriage and Divorce Act:

Note to page 54   171

The court shall determine custody in accordance with the best interests of the child. The court shall consider all relevant factors including:

(1) the wishes of the child's parent or parents as to his custody;

(2) the wishes of the child as to his custodian;

(3) the interaction and interrelationship of the child with his parent or parents, his siblings, and any other person who may significantly affect the child's best interests;

(4) the child's adjustment to his home, school, and community; and

(5) the mental and physical health of all individuals involved.

To this general codification of existing law the drafters of the Uniform Act have added:

The court shall not consider conduct of a proposed custodian that does not affect his relationship to the child.

And see, e.g., Judge Dye's dissent in *In re Jewish Child Care Association*, 5 N.Y. 2d 222, 156 N.E. 2d 700 (1957):

In sustaining petitioner's application for a writ of habeas corpus, a majority of this court is about to say that the best interest of the infant will be served by compelling the approved foster parents, with whom the petitioner had previously placed the child for custodial care, to surrender her back to the Agency, there to be dealt with as they see fit. This tragic result comes about because of a mistaken notion that the courts are bound to accept an administrative policy of the Agency as controlling their determination rather than to exercise their own traditional power and authority in accordance with the evidence. While administrative practices have a useful place in the handling of ordinary matters of administration, such test is wholly inappropriate in this setting. Here we are not dealing with a routine problem of administration, but rather with the fundamental concept underlying the broad and enlightened social welfare program of the State respecting the care and custody of indigent and neglected children, every aspect of which is to be tested in the light of which will best promote their individual welfare. . . . There came a time when the foster parents proposed adoption, first to the caseworker who disapproved, then to the grandmother, and finally to the mother herself, who temporized and declined to give any definite answer which is regarded as a refusal. The Agency did not like the emotional development as it was their policy to keep the care children in a neutral environment—where there could be no "pull on the child between her loyalty to her foster parents and her mother". To this policy the Agency required the foster parents, as a condition of continued custody, to sign a paper declaring that they understood that Laura could

"remain only with the status of a foster child".
However, this failed of its intended purpose.

And see dissent of Judge Froessel:

> The Agency took the position, at the
> hearing, that it could not function properly if a
> "foster family was in position to question our
> judgment, even if our judgment, if you weigh it,
> might turn out to be wrong". Perhaps they are
> right (Social Welfare Law, § 383). . . . I am of
> the opinion that the Agency, however well moti-
> vated, has committed grave error here, contrary
> to the best interests of the child; that the courts
> below were in no small measure erroneously
> influenced by the so-called rights of the Agency,
> rather than by the welfare of the child.

2. In Chapter 1 we assert our value preference for a state
   policy which prefers the child's over any adult interest
   whenever the child's placement becomes the subject of
   controversy. We develop this position more fully in
   Chapter 8.

3. *Re W* (an infant) [1970] *3 All E.R.* 990 and [1971]
   2 All E.R. 49.

4. [1970] *3 All E.R.*, p. 996.

5. *Ibid.*

6. *Ibid.*, p. 1006.

7. *Ibid.*, p. 1002.

8. [1971] *2 All E.R.*, pp. 55, 56, 59.

9. With the substitution of the least detrimental alternative
    standard such an Act might also provide, as does the
    Virginia Code §63.1 225 after setting forth what parties
    must ordinarily consent to adoption:

    > (4) If after hearing evidence the court finds that the
    >   consent of any person or agency whose consent is
    >   hereinabove required is withheld contrary to the
    >   best interests of the child, or if a valid consent
    >   is unobtainable, the court may grant the petition
    >   without such consent.

    Our value preference for minimum state inter-
    vention would dictate against such an exception to initial
    consent on the assumption that neglect, abandonment,
    and other such provisions should be adequate to remove
    children from their adult custodians and to place them
    for adoption without the consent of such adults in such
    extreme cases.

    See also *In re Lem,* cited in Chapter 3, note **18**
    (*supra*).

10. Had the House of Lords affirmed the Appellate Court's
    view of the law, as it might well have, it would have de-
    stroyed the developing relationship between *W* and his
    adopting parents. With the least detrimental alternative
    as the guideline under the new Act, the review courts
    would have been denied such power. At most, should the
    lengthy review procedure continue to be authorized, ap-
    pellate authority should go only to making *prospective*
    rulings in such cases. If review courts after such lapses
    of time are not limited to applying their rulings to future
    cases, the particular child's interest is subordinated to a

court policy which in general, but not in this specific case, may be in the child's best interest.

11. In Juvenile delinquency proceedings involving violent conduct, even if the law were to make society's immediate safety the primary goal, we would argue that within that ambit the least detrimental alternative placement should be selected for the child.

12. A judicially supervised drawing of lots between two equally acceptable psychological parents might be the most rational and least offensive process for resolving the hard choice.

Dealing with another matter, B. Currie, in *Selected Essays on the Conflicts of Laws* (Durham, N.C.: Duke University Press, 1963, pp. 120–121), wrote:

> Application of the law of the place of making [of the contract: the "traditional approach] means that the disinterested third state would casually defeat the one and now the other policy, depending upon a purely fortuitous circumstance. One is almost tempted to suggest that it would be better to flip a coin, since that procedure would produce the same result more economically.
>
> It will be said this is a "give-it-up" philosophy. Of course it is. A give-it-up attitude is constructive when it appears that the task is impossible of accomplishment with the resources that are available. It would have been constructive if geometricians had given up long before they did the effort to square the circle by means of a straightedge and compass

Likewise, dealing with another matter concerned with legislative motive, J. H. Ely, in "Motivation in Constitutional Law," 79 *Yale Law J.*, 1234 n. 97 (1970), cites the following passage by John Barth which is apposite to the problem we pose:

> If the alternatives are side by side, choose the one on the left; if they're consecutive in time, choose the earlier. If neither of these applies, choose the alternative whose name begins with the earlier letter of the alphabet. These are the principles of Sinistrality, Antecedence, and Alphabetical Priority—there are others, and they're arbitrary, but useful [J. Barth, *The End of the Road*, New York: Bantam Books, 1969, p. 85].

CHAPTER 5:   ON PARTY STATUS AND THE RIGHT TO REPRESENTATION

1. See *Shields* v. *Barrow* 58 U.S. 130, 139 (1854) for the now classic statement of Mr. Justice Curtis on party status:

> The court here points out three classes of parties to a bill in equity. They are: 1. Formal parties. 2. Persons having an interest in the controversy, and who ought to be made parties, in order that the court may act on that rule which requires it to decide on, and finally determine the entire controversy, and do complete justice, by adjusting all the rights involved in it. These persons are commonly termed necessary parties; but if their interests are separable from those of

the parties before the court, so that the court can proceed to a decree, and do complete and final justice, without affecting other persons not before the court, the latter are not indispensable parties. 3. Persons who not only have an interest in the controversy, but an interest of such a nature that a final decree cannot be made without either affecting that interest, or leaving the controversy in such a condition that its final termination may be wholly inconsistent with equity and good conscience.

2.   See *In re Gault* 387 U.S. 1 (1967) which holds that a child in delinquency proceedings (which is a placement procedure) is entitled to counsel.

The juvenile needs the assistance of counsel to cope with problems of law, to make skilled inquiry into the facts, to insist upon regularity of the proceedings, and to ascertain whether he has a defense and to prepare and submit it [*id.* at 36].

3.   And see *Wisconsin* v. *Yoder*, 406 U.S. 205 (1972) holding that the State's claim that it is empowered as *parens patriae* to compel attendance at secondary schools of children against their parents' wishes could not be sustained against their claim as Amish to the free exercise of their religion.

Justice Douglas dissenting in part because the children were not consulted observed:

I agree with the Court that the religious scruples of the Amish are opposed to the education of their children beyond the grade schools, yet I disagree with the Court's conclusion that the matter is within the dispensation of parents alone. . . .

These children are "persons" within the meaning of the Bill of Rights. We have so held over and over again. . . .

While the parents, absent dissent, normally speak for the entire family, the education of the child is a matter on which the child will often have decided views. . . .

4. See Jeremy Bentham, *Theory of Legislation* (Volume I, 1840, *supra*, pp. 252–253):

[A] father is, in some respects, the master, in others, the guardian of the child. . . .

Under the first relation, the advantage of the father is considered; under the second, that of the child. These two relations are easily reconciled in the person of the father, on account of his natural affection, which leads him much rather to make sacrifices on account of his children, than to avail himself of his rights for his own advantage.

It would seem, at the first glance, that the legislator need not interfere between fathers and children; that he might trust to the tenderness of the parent, and the gratitude of the child. But this superficial view would be deceptive. It is absolutely necessary, on one side, to limit the paternal power, and on the other, to maintain filial respect by legal enactments.

5. The Uniform Marriage and Divorce Act provides:

> The court may appoint an attorney to
> represent the interests of a minor or dependent
> child with respect to his custody, support, and
> visitation. The court shall enter an order for
> costs, fees and disbursements in favor of the
> child's attorney. The order shall be made against
> either or both parents, except that, if the respon-
> sible party is indigent, the costs, fees, and dis-
> bursements shall be borne by the [appropriate
> agency].

CHAPTER 6:   THE ROTHMAN DECISIONS

1. Art Buchwald, the distinguished humorist, who fifty
years ago was a foster child, recalled in a speech cele-
brating the 150th Anniversary of the Jewish Child Care
Association in April, 1972 (unpublished):

> The status of a foster child, particularly
> for the foster child, is a strange one. He's part
> of a no-man's land.
>   . . . The child knows instinctively that
> there is nothing permanent about the setup, and
> he is, so to speak, on loan to the family he is
> residing with. If it doesn't work out, he can be
> swooped up and put in another home.
>   It's pretty hard to ask a child or foster
> parent to make a large emotional commitment
> under these conditions, and so I think I was
> about seven years old, when confused, lonely
> and terribly insecure I said to myself, "The hell
> with it. I think I'll become a humorist."

From then on I turned everything into a joke. Starting as the class clown, I graduated to making fun of all authority figures from the principal of the school to the social service worker who visited every month. When a person is grown up and he attacks authority, society pays him large sums of money. But when he's a kid and he makes fun of authority, they beat his brains in.

Having chosen this dangerous pastime of getting attention by poking fun at everything, I found I could survive. I had my bag of laughs, and I had my fantasies, which I must say were really great. Would you believe that I dreamed I was really the son of a Rothschild, and I was kidnapped by gypsies when I was six months old, and sold to a couple who were going to America?

If you believe that, would you believe the Rothschilds had hired France's foremost detective to find me and that it was only a matter of time when he would trace me to the foster home in Hollis, Long Island, and would you believe that once my true identity had been established, I would prevail on my Rothschild father to drop all charges against the people that had kidnapped me, and give them a substantial pension?

That's the kind of kid my social worker had to deal with.

2.   This should read: Council of Child Psychiatry.

CHAPTER 7:   PROVISIONS FOR A CHILD PLACEMENT STATUTE

1. Draftsmen of codes can easily identify what parts of the text are most directly related to each section.

CHAPTER 8:   WHY SHOULD THE CHILD'S INTERESTS BE PARAMOUNT?

1. With regard to delinquency, see, e.g., N. Morris and G. Hawkins, *The Honest Politician's Guide to Crime Control* (Chicago: University of Chicago Press, 1970, pp. 146–147):

> Conditions included in the various statutory descriptions of delinquent behavior comprise a medley consisting of anything from smoking cigarettes, truancy, sleeping in alleys, and using vulgar language to major felonies such as rape and homicide. Moreover, such vague, imprecise, and subjective terms as idleness, loitering, waywardness, stubbornness, incorrigibility, and immoral conduct are commonly employed: concepts so loose that, as Paul Tappan has observed, "to many they may appear to describe the normal behavior of the little-inhibited and non-neurotic child." Indeed, there must be few children who do not at one time or another engage in behavior that is somewhere defined as delinquent.

See also Note, "Parens Patriae and Statutory Vagueness in the Juvenile Court," 82 *Yale Law J.* 745 (1973).

The same may be said of neglect provisions.

2. A recent case of mistaken identification in the newborn nursery attests to how little attention is given to the child's rights when the adults place biological reality and continuity ahead of psychological reality and continuity.

As reported in the *Japan Times* (Saturday, May 26, 1973), a routine blood-typing of an eleven-year-old boy enrolling at an elementary school revealed that he was not the biological child of his parents. This led to the reconstruction of a mixup in the newborn nursery in which there was an unwitting exchange of two baby boys, which was revealed accidentally eleven years later.

According to the *Japan Times*, "It has been agreed by the parties concerned that the boys be returned to their proper parents after a certain period of familiarization during which both families get together."

This statement suggests that the two boys are not concerned parties compared to the adults. Also, it indicates that the parents' conviction about the importance of the blood line, that is, the biological relationship (as revealed by the routine laboratory finding), overrides the mutual psychological ties that both they and the children must have formed in the period of eleven years.

Initially we might be inclined to conclude that the state should safeguard the existing, ongoing, psychological parent-child relationships by finding that an adoption by common law has taken place.

But these are not contested placement cases. Both families wish to make the transfer. Thus, to accord with our value preference for minimum state intervention and with our guideline which recognizes the limits of the law—i.e., that the state cannot force personal relationships to continue if any one of the parties to the relationship want to alter or break it—the state should not intrude on the private rearrangement of these relationships. It must be recognized that each child is no longer "wanted" by the family in which he finds himself but rather is wanted by the family to which he "belongs" by blood-tie. To the extent that the families seek assistance in the transfer they should be encouraged—as they apparently plan to do—to make the transition gradually and with understanding for the difficulties it will cause the children.

However, if one of the families objected to making the switch, we would have a contested child placement and the ongoing parent-child relationship should be protected in that family which objects to switching. Whether the other child would continue to be unwanted in his present family or whether the blood-tie family would want to adopt him presents another setting in which the least detrimental alternative would have to be found.

3. Letter of November 27, 1972, from Professor L. de Jong, Director, Netherlands State Institute for War Documentation. The authors are grateful to Dr. L. de Jong for summarizing these data and for making the information available.

EPILOGUE: FURTHER OBSERVATIONS ON THE APPLICATION OF THE LEAST DETRIMENTAL ALTERNATIVE STANDARD

1. On the functions of the disposition stage of decision as well as of the invocation and adjudication stages in the

child placement process, see Joseph Goldstein, Anna
Freud, and Albert J. Solnit, *Before the Best Interests of
the Child* (New York: Free Press, Chapter 2, 1979)
(hereinafter cited as *Before the Best Interests of the
Child*).

2.   83 *Yale Law J.* 1304 (1974).

3.   On short-term temporary foster care see *Before the Best
Interests of the Child* (Chapter 4 note 15, and accompanying text).

4.   See, e.g., N. Dembitz, "Beyond Any Discipline's Competence," 83 *Yale Law J.* 1304, 1310 (1974); Richard S.
Benedek and Elissa P. Benedek, "Postdivorce Visitation:
A Child's Right" (*Journal of the American Academy of
Child Psychiatry*, 16:256–271, 1977); and Strauss and
Strauss, "Book Review," 74 *Columbia Law Rev.* 996, 1004
(1974). On visitation or access as "a basic right of the
child rather than a basic right of the [noncustodial]
parent see *M* v *M* [1973] 2 A11 E R 81 (Family Div.).

5.   See pp. 37–38, 49–50, and 101.

6.   See *Before the Best Interests of the Child* (Chapter 4).

7.   See, *e.g., Grado* v. *Grado*, 44 A.D.2d 854, 356 N.Y.S. 2d
85 (1974) where the visitation order provided as follows:
         Every second and fourth weekend;
         Every first and third Saturday from 10:00 AM to
            7:30 PM;

> Every first and third Sunday from 10:00 AM to
>   11:00 AM;
> Every Monday from 6:00 PM to 8:30 PM;
> Every Wednesday from 6:00 PM to 9:30 PM;
> Every holiday;
> Two weeks during the summer.

(Reprinted from Judge Cooper's unreported opinion in the same case, Docket No. R 13390/73 Family Court of the State of New York, City of New York: County of Kings, p. 4.)

8. We favor contact between a child and his noncustodial parent so long as neither parent can use the courts to force the other to arrange visits. Even if requested by both parents, we would object to courts making a visitation agreement a part of its decree. If mere registration were to give both parents a greater sense of commitment to make visitation work, a visitation certificate with no more than symbolic force might be issued to them. As an alternative, it might be desirable for courts to add to their unconditional custody awards an appropriate paraphrase of the state's WARNING to cigarette smokers:

> DENIAL OF VISITS MAY BE
> DETRIMENTAL TO YOUR CHILD.

Out of concern for equalizing the bargaining strength of separating parents Mnookin and Kornhauser argue that visitation and joint custody agreements should be specifically enforceable in law. Their faith in the law's capacity to implement such contracts in situations where the law has already proved powerless to enforce marriage contracts seems ludicrous. The marriage contract is now generally construed to mean "till divorce do us part." It is a "binding" contract until either spouse wants out. Even if visitation is retained as a "bargaining chip," joint custody and visitation agreements will ultimately come to mean—at enormous cost to the children involved—specifically enforceable until either the custodial or noncustodial parent wants out. In any event, Mnookin and Kornhauser fail to make the child's interests paramount in their argument. R. H. Mnookin and L. Kornhauser, "Bargaining in the Shadow of the Law: The Case of Divorce," 88 *Yale Law J.* 950, 980–984 (1979).

9. For a conflicting view, see J. B. Kelly and J. S. Wallerstein, "The Effects of Parental Divorce: Experiences of the Child in Early Latency" (*American Journal of Orthopsychiatry*, 46:20–32, 1976); J. S. Wallerstein and J. B. Kelly, "Divorce Counselling: A Community Service for Families in the Midst of Divorce" (*ibid.*, 47:4–22, 1977); and J. S. Wallerstein and J. B. Kelly, "The Effects of Parental Divorce: Experiences of the Preschool Child" (*Journal of the American Academy of Child Psychiatry*, 14:600–616, 1975).

10. *Braiman* v. *Braiman*, 378 N.E.2d 1019, 1020 (1978).

11. *Id.* at 1021 and 1022.

12. On joint custody, see Annot., " 'Split,' 'Divided,' or 'Alternate' Custody of Children," 92 A.L.R.2d 695 (1963).

13. See note 4.

14. But see *B* v. *B* (1971), 3 All E.R. 682, in which the court

affirms a lower court decision to deny a noncustodial father access to his sixteen-year-old son:

> I can say without any hesitation that I feel the greatest sympathy with the father in this case. I think that in the events that have happened he has probably had a 'raw deal', if I may use a slang expression. He rightly points out that the conclusion of the Official Solicitor is that really the mother and grandfather have shut the door in his face with regard to this boy. But the damage is done. It would not be proper for this court to make an order for access to reward the father or to punish the mother. We have got to consider what is best for this boy. The learned judge, having heard the arguments put forward by the father and having heard the evidence of the psychiatrist, Dr. Heller, who was called to give oral evidence, came to the conclusion that it would do no good at all for this boy to be forced against his will to go and see his father; on the contrary, it might well do him harm (Davies LJ.) [*id.* at 688].

And see N. Turner, "Wardship: The Official Solicitor's Role" (*Journal of the Association of British Adoption and Fostering Agencies,* p. 30, 34, 1977):

> [I do not like to be brought into a case] where a child is obdurate in refusing to see a parent entitled to access notwithstanding all the skill of the judge and of the welfare officers inevitably concerned. Hopes that if I am brought in my

staff may be able to do something are likely to
be disappointed, and my intervention may do
more harm than good. A case of this type,
Taylor v. Taylor was before the Court of Appeal in 1975 and is reported in *Family Law*
for that year at p 151. I wish sometimes it were
more widely known.

15. See *Sorichetti* v. *City of New York*, 4 F.L.R. 2635 (Aug.
15, 1978) involving suit by a custodial parent against the
New York City police department for its failure to enforce a protection order against her estranged husband.
When she delivered her daughter for the ordered visitation, he threatened the daughter's life. She then informed
the police of his threats, showed them the protection
order, and requested their assistance. It was denied. Later
the father attempted to murder the child who was found
mutilated and disfigured. And see Chapter 5 in *Before the
Best Interests of the Child,* concerning the *Gray* case
where the court ordered overnight visits for children with
their mother who had been acquitted by reason of in-
sanity of attempting to murder them.

For another example of simplistic but logical
thinking about visitation see *C.M.* v. *C.C.*, 152 N.J. 160,
377 A2d 821 (1977), granting visitation rights to the
donor of semen for a child conceived by artificial insemination:

In this case there is a known man who is
the donor. There is no husband. If the couple had
been married and the husband's sperm was used
artificially, he would be considered the father. If

a woman conceives a child by intercourse, the "donor" who is not married to the mother is no less a father than the man who is married to the mother. Likewise, if an unmarried woman conceives a child through artificial insemination from semen from a known man, that man cannot be considered to be less a father because he is not married to the woman.

* * *

It is in a child's best interests to have two parents whenever possible. The court takes no position as to the propriety of the use of artificial insemination between unmarried persons, but must be concerned with the best interests of the child in granting custody or visitation, and for such consideration will not make any distinction between a child conceived naturally or artificially.

Index

A

Abandonment, 5, 7, 12, 17, 22, 33–34, 36, 47–49, 55, 58, 109, 174
  evidence for, 48–49, 105, 167–68
  involuntary, 107–11
  psychological, 48–49, 77–79, 82–83, 166–67
Abuse, 17, 36, 105, 149
Access, *see* Visitation
Adjudication, 184
Adolescent, 19, 23, 34, 41
Adopted child, search for real parent, 23, 140–41
Adoption, 5–7, 16, 21–23, 32, 107
  annulment of, 37, 128–29
  common-law, 26–28, 108
  conditional, 23, 117, 148–49
  consent, 22, 37, 55–61, 138–39, 161, 174
  contested, 55–62, 66
  "de facto" ("virtual," "equitable"), 145
  eligibility for, 47–48
  finality, 22, 35–37, 46, 138–39, 149–50
  "matching" child and parent, 23, 139
  motives for, 22–23
  period of appeal, 37, 46; *see also* Time, child's sense of
  procedures leaving parent–child relationship uncertain, 6, 22, 61–63, 138–39
  religious conditions, 139, 150
  residency requirements, 139
  subsidized, 39, 157–59
  unconditional, 35–37
  waiting period, 22, 35–37, 45–46, 150–51
  see also Continuity of relationship, Custody, Foster care, Time
Adoption Act (England), 55, 58, 61
Adoption Act, Uniform, 116–18, 128–30
Adoptive parent, 7, 19, 116
  common-law, 7, 27–28, 39, 48, 79–80, 98, 108
  definition, 22–23, 98
Adults
  affectionate tie to child, 16–

193

Cooper v. *Aaron*, 164
Court
  acts quickly to safeguard
    child's physical well-
    being, 43–44, 164
  adult-centered, 55, 106–07
  authority versus capacity
    to do, 114–15
  need for speedy procedures,
    46, 55, 62–63, 101; *see
    also* Child placement;
    Time, child's sense of
  as *parens patriae*, 115, 133
  should not retain jurisdic-
    tion over child–parent
    relationship, 101
Criminal, 34, 148–49
Cross, Lord Justice, 57
Culpability, 79–80
Currie, B., 175
Curtis, Justice, 176–77
Custody
  appeals, 37–39, 47, 101,
    151–55
  conditions, 6, 37–38, 114–33
  decisions, 6, 37–39, 114–16,
    152–55
  denial of, 110
  divided, 120, 186
  in divorce (and separation),
    5, 6, 28, 37–39, 46–47, 62–
    63, 98, 100
  joint, 120, 185–86
  judicial drawing of lots,
    155–56
  need for speedy procedures,
    45–47, 55, 62–63, 101, 165

  not subject to court modifi-
    cation, 98–101
  review, 62–63, 174–75
  split, 6, 120, 186
  subject to court modifica-
    tion, 6, 37–39, 62–63,
    129–33, 166, 170–73
  unconditional, 38–39, 63,
    101
  see also Adoption, Foster
    care, Visitation

D

Davis adoption case, 168
Davis, Lord Justice, 187
de Jong, L., xiii, 183
Delinquency, juvenile, 4, 5,
  16, 34
  determination of, 105, 181
  proceedings, 62, 65, 125,
    175, 177
Dembitz, N., Judge, 113–14,
  184
Desramault case, 154–55
Disposition, 113, 117, 183–84
Divorce, 5, 21, 28, 37–39, 46–
  47, 62–63, 66, 98, 100,
  110, 153–55, 178–79
  denial of, does not establish
    healthy marriage, 169
  divisible, 165–66
  see also Custody, Visitation
Domestic relations law, 149–
  50
Donnelly, R. C., 147